T0311558

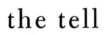

the tell

the tell

⌒ a memoir ⌒

LINDA I. MEYERS

SHE WRITES PRESS

Published June 5, 2018
Printed in the United States of America
Print ISBN: 978-1-63152-355-7
E-ISBN: 978-1-63152-356-4
Library of Congress Control Number: 2018930510

For information, address:
She Writes Press
1563 Solano Ave #546
Berkeley, CA 94707

Interior design by Tabitha Lahr

She Writes Press is a division of SparkPoint Studio, LLC.

Names and identifying characteristics have been changed to protect the privacy of certain individuals.

My grandmother Eva Stone,

My sons David, Jonathan, and Robert,

My grandchildren Sjoen, Maple, and George:

THIS BOOK IS FOR YOU.

contents

Author's Foreword....9

The Afikomen....11

The Jewels in the Salt....13

The Flowers....21

When They Were Eight....33

Negative Space....49

Putting the Pieces Together....55

Outside the Frame....71

To the Mountain....79

A Photo Left Out in the Sun....99

Dr. Zhivago....111

Had I Won at Bingo....119

Dead Serious....129

Feng Shui in the *Shtetl*....143

Sharks and Other Perils....157

Running It Over Again....171

The Hand Off....183

My Name Is Linda....197

The Spring Line....217

Acknowledgments....227

About the Author....229

author's foreword

A tell is an unconscious reveal given under psychological stress. The poker player who recognizes an opponent's tell, perhaps the twitch of the eye or the soft intake of breath, is best situated to win the game or, at the least, to mitigate her losses. A tell is also an archaeological mound containing the accumulated remains of human occupation and abandonment over many centuries. And a telltale or tattletale is a child who reports others' wrongdoings or reveals their secrets.

This memoir is a tell in all of its meanings. It is a compilation of standalone essays that together trace my journey out of the tell my family inhabited and through the restrictive and chauvinistic culture of the forties and fifties, towards emancipation and self-realization. The essays about the generations that came before me are written in third person. Once I'm able to speak for myself, the book moves into first person. I have selected only those episodes from my life that I believe to be turning points and best tell this story; therefore, large sections of time are intentionally left out.

Louise and Linda age four

⌒ the afikomen ⌒

My cousin Louise and I were tired of sitting "nicely" at my grandmother Pauline's seder table and waiting for Uncle Harry to plow through the *entire* Passover Haggahdah. At some undefined moment, we gave each other a knowing eye and slipped under the table to wait it out. Every few minutes, I pulled on my father's pant leg, and he handed me down some matzah and celery sticks—impossible to eat without a loud crunch. We tried to stifle our giggles, but my mother heard them and gave us little kicks that said *quiet down.* When it was time to ask the first of the four seder questions, we resurfaced.

"Why is this night different from other nights?" Louise's little brother Allen would say in his singsong voice.

The question I wanted to ask was not in the Haggahdah. I wanted to know *why would that night be the same as any other night?* Meaning my parents' inevitable fight on the way home, the silence in the morning, the pots banging over breakfast, the blowup, the slammed door, the threats. I'd come to know the pattern, but I didn't understand the cause.

The best part of the Passover seder was the search at the end for the afikomen—the hidden matzah. Louise was always excited to find the matzah and get the money, but I was more into the search—the license to rifle through drawers and closets in my grandmother's bedroom. The prize for me was not the money, but clues to my father's past—snapshots, postcards, mementoes, anything that might answer the *why*.

From the time I could read fairy tales and dream of happily ever after, I wanted to understand my parents. Who had they been before they met? What had attracted them to each other? What mitigating circumstances in their lives might explain the disaster that was their marriage, and the sadness that was my legacy? Like Nancy Drew, I was always on the hunt for clues to solve the mystery. I learned to look in unlikely places and to listen for the unspoken truth. I became expert at reading facial expressions and watching for the *tell*—the unconscious wrinkle of the nose or raise of the eyebrow that gave away the lie. If I could understand the *why*, I might figure out the *how*—how to fix it.

After the afikomen was found and Louise collected her two dollars, we slid back under the table where I listened to the grownups tell their unabridged versions of the past. My imagination brought the stories I heard to life. Together with the scenes I witnessed, books I read, and movies I saw, I constructed a narrative that helped me understand my family, and the people who came before us.

the jewels in the salt

S aratoga Avenue ran into Livonia, and Livonia intersected with Amboy. Once you turned right on Amboy, the club was only a few storefronts away. It was after dinner, and the Brooklyn streets were clogged with kids getting in their last game of stickball and peddlers wrapping up their wares for the night. He wove his way through the glut, careful not to brush into anyone or step in any horse droppings. He wore the black pinstripe—Isaac, the tailor, had pegged the pants exactly how he told him, but the Chinaman had overstarched the collar of the shirt, and he had to keep stretching his neck to loosen it.

He had taken his father's gold cufflinks for the night. He'd wished she'd give them to him already. He felt like an ass every time, trying to dig them out of the box of kosher salt. That was his mother's idea of a place for safekeeping. He was sure there was some sort of irony to the jewels in the salt, but he'd long ago stopped trying to figure her out. He concentrated again on tonight and getting to the club. That's where the action was going to be.

He was walking fast, but not so fast that he couldn't take a minute to check himself out in the window of the butcher shop. He wedged his image between the hanging sides of beef. He had a strong chin, dark, wavy hair, and what they call "bedroom" eyes. He knew when he got to the club that she'd be waiting for him to show and trying to act as if she couldn't care less.

Having served and cleaned up dinner, the women on Saratoga were finally released from the kitchen. They sat, lining the stoops in flowered housedresses, stockings rolled down to their ankles. George thought they looked like a bunch of overpotted plants—Brownsville shrubbery—with not enough light and too little water. He had to look closely to see that some of them were no older than he was. It didn't matter, because, once they married and the kids started to come, they became indentured servants to the next generation. Look at them. What a shame! They could sit there from today to tomorrow with their hair in curlers, and they'd still be no one you'd want to wake up to in the morning. His mother never sat on the stoop. He had to give her that.

Usually he'd stop and give them the time of day, but he was in a hurry. Gussie, the one who'd had to put her oldest in an orphanage, yelled after him. "Georgie, how are ya? How you doin', Georgie? How's your mother? So beautiful, your mother. Gorgeous, I'm telling you. Such a pity about your father. What is it, ten years? You were eight, weren't ya, Georgie?" And then Gussie would turn to Edna to help make her case. "Edna, look at Georgie. Look at him. Isn't he the spittin' image of Louie? You look just like your father, Georgie. He'd be proud."

That's what they said to his face, but, as soon as they thought he was out of earshot, they'd whisper how he'd gone bad, and how Pauline must be pulling her hair out watching him run the streets. "That's the problem," Gussie would say to Edna. "She let him run the streets."

"What was she supposed to do?" asked Edna, "She's working to make ends meet, taking care of her sister's kids. You heard about her sister Sarah. She has time? What would you do, Gussie? Ah, who am I asking? I know what you'd do. You did it."

"Yeah, so," said Gussie. "Better he should run the streets." And by then they'd forgotten Georgie, and they'd argue until one or the other would go back inside and slam the door.

And so they'd serve him up—first a smile and then a whack. He didn't care; at least he was talked about. Hey, he'd rather be a light than a lamppost. He'd read that somewhere. Where had he read that? Some book . . . he couldn't remember. He'd quit school when he was sixteen. It's not that he wasn't smart. He was plenty smart. He could have stayed. Graduated. But time was money. He wasn't reading books, but he was learning how to turn nickels into quarters and quarters into dollars. He was learning that it didn't matter *what* you know but *who* you know, and he was a fast learner. He wouldn't admit it to anyone, but he still wished he could remember that book.

When he hit Pitkin, he turned right and walked under the El. He passed Shlomo's Deli and reached into the barrel, grabbing a sour pickle. He shook off the juice so it wouldn't drip on his shirt. Shlomo looked out at him, raised his arm, and rubbed his two fingers together, making the sign of money. This was their joke. He'd been stealing pickles from Shlomo since he was six. He smiled at Shlomo, waved, and kept walking. Shlomo threw up his hands—he never knew what to do about Georgie.

As he got closer to the club, George became Gerry, the name that all the Dukes called him. There were two cellar clubs on Sutter, one new one where the guys were still trying to figure out what to call themselves, and then the Sutter Kings, a bunch of wops, one chink, and three white guys lucky to have somewhere to go on a Saturday night. Some of the Dukes worried about the Kings. Sammy in particular would go three blocks out of his way rather than walk down Sutter. Sammy was an ass. "What are they gonna do to you, Sammy?" George would ask. "Kill you? They lay a hand on you and they'll get whacked by Lepke. They ain't gonna mess with Lepke."

If Lepke had you in his pocket, you could walk all over Brooklyn, and nobody would touch you. Maybe George was in Lepke's pocket, but no one knew how he got there. They didn't ask. They were afraid to know, so they chalked it up to his charm. "Hey, come on. What are you, kiddin' me? This guy could charm the skin off a snake." Then they'd all agree that even without Lepke, Gerry still deserved to be their president. If it weren't for him, the Amboy Dukes would be nothing, just another bunch of Brooklyn bums trying to look like big shots.

When he turned onto Amboy, he could hear Jimmy Dorsey blasting from the record player. He saw the crowd hanging by the door of the club. Initiation into the Dukes was like taking communion; you got to pick the name you wanted. George had picked Gerry. No one knew why about that either. They thought he would have picked Louie like his father, but Lepke was Louie. He wanted to be Gerry, so who was going to argue.

Stella was standing near the railing with Mike. George liked Stella. She would have been pretty if she'd have left herself alone, but the dress was too tight, the heels were too high, and the hair was too big. By the time she'd finished with herself, she looked like a floozy.

"Hi, Gerry. Where you going tonight?" she purred. "Hey Mikey, get a load of Gerry. Why don't you ever wear a suit, Mikey? You'd look good in a suit, but not as good as Gerry."

She was playing to him. For two weeks, she'd been trying to get in the door, but Gerry kept telling her the place was too crowded. "Maybe if you cut your hair you could fit in the room," he'd tease her, but he really wished he could get her to tone it down. She was wasting herself.

He looked over at Mike. "What do you say, Mike, we got room for Stella tonight?" Stella backed her ass into Mike's hand until he smiled and said, "Okay."

The Dukes paid Manny the landlord fifty bucks a month. Manny was charging more than he should, but Gerry told the guys it was still a deal. Manny didn't bother them. The tenants complained about the racket till all hours, and Manny ignored them. He knew the Dukes were in with Lepke, and they could have paid him nothing, and there would have been nothing he could do about it. Gerry believed you get what you pay for. He wasn't going to shaft Manny. Fair was fair.

The club was packed. It was late enough that the guys had turned down the lights, and the PRIVACY sign was already up on the door to the back room, but he spotted her immediately. She was in the corner, talking to Sammy. He breathed a sigh of relief. The pinstripe wasn't going to be for nothing.

He'd first met her the week before at the Palladium when he'd gone to watch the marathon. He was a good dancer, but he was damned if he was going to dance for hours and hours just to raise money for some charity. He'd rather put his feet up and write a check, but two of the Dukes were dancing, and he'd promised them he'd come watch. He saw her out there. The band was playing a jitterbug. And her partner was throwing her over his head and pulling her between his legs. She was good. They were probably the best dancers on the floor. He asked Zig if he knew who she was, and Zig said her name was Tillie and she lived over on Schenck Avenue. She didn't look like she lived on Schenck. Schenck was on the border between Brownsville and East New York. "Yeah," Zig said, "she lives on Schenck, and she went to Jefferson High School." Gerry didn't think he'd ever seen her at school, or he would've remembered. Zig said she used to go out with Big Al, but he laughed and guessed that Al wasn't big enough, 'cause she'd dumped him.

When she finally gave it up and walked off the dance floor, he'd gone over. "I'm Gerry," he said, "and you are one hell of a dancer." She thanked him and said he didn't need to introduce himself; she knew who he was. When he asked how, she just smiled. She had the kind of beauty that didn't shout out at you. Gerry thought that even though she lived on Schenck, she still looked like money. She said her name was Tessie.

"I was Tillie when I was a baby. Now, I'm Tessie. I like Tessie better. You can understand that, *Georgie*, can't you?" She gave him a coy smile. He invited her to come down to the club on Saturday night. He promised her it was the best gig in Brooklyn, and he'd give her a good time. She said she'd see—she might have something else to do.

"She'll make it," he'd said to Zig when they were getting into the car, but he wasn't that sure.

He waited at the bar until he thought she was finally tired of pretending he wasn't there, and then he walked over and handed her a drink. She switched her cigarette to her other hand and took it. Her nonchalance was the draw. The other girls were wearing tight dresses. They kept bending down to straighten their seams, but Tessie didn't have to work to look good. She was wearing tan slacks that draped loosely over her hips. She had on a green silk blouse with a neckline that dipped deep enough that you could see a little lace peeping out from her bra.

"Thanks for the drink."

"You are very, very welcome," he said, giving her the smile that usually knocked them dead. And then he waited. He'd learned that the girls couldn't stand the silence, and, if you waited, they'd do all the talking, but she said nothing. She sipped her drink, and when her eyes began to wander around the room, he panicked and started throwing her the story about the club and how the Amboy Dukes were the best club in Brooklyn. He was trying not to give her the spiel, but she was making him lose his calm, and he was coming up empty. He was about to tell her to piss off when she put her cigarette out in her drink, handed him the glass, and politely excused herself. He watched her walk away and thought, *This girl is a dish. She's got enough style and class, if she wanted, she could be one of Lepke's girls.*

He'd ask Zig where on Schenck she lived, and he'd send her flowers. He wasn't giving up so easy.

And that was how George met Tillie, Gerry met Tessie, my father met my mother.

Grandparents, Eva & Harry, Wedding

᧑ the flowers ᧒

Eva stood at the sink scrubbing the scales off the fish. She did not look down at her work; her hands had long ago memorized the task. She concentrated on the spidery pattern of cracks on the tiles in front of her. From behind, Eva looked like a young woman—her back was straight, her hair was mostly black, and the bulbous veins that ran up her legs from too much time on her feet were hidden under her stockings—but when she turned, her face gave away her age. Years of furrowing her brow had burrowed deep lines of skepticism between her eyes. Pursing her lips had drawn fine little lines that radiated out from the corners of her mouth like a child's drawing of the sun.

Eva accepted her looks. She was forty-two, after all, and had never been a beauty. Believing that waste was a sin, she did what she could with what she had. Mineral oil was her elixir. Each night she poured three tablespoons into a cup—two she drank to squelch the heartburn, and the third she rubbed on her face to smooth out the lines and give her skin a youthful luster. It was the nightly application of mineral oil that made her skin like satin, but it was her thoughts of Malconson that gave her the young girl's blush.

Eva knew that Malconson thought she was a fine-looking woman. She could tell by the way he peeked at her over his cards and reached out to touch her arm when she offered him tea or another piece of mandel bread.

Malconson was a tall man. Eva, an expert seamstress, was able to estimate yardage by simply looking at the fabric. She would tell you that Malconson was five feet ten or eleven. An inch here or an inch there didn't matter; Eva was happy to have a man she could look up to. There was little about Malconson she didn't admire. His temperament was in the sweetness of his face. When he smiled at her, he poured honey on her heart. He was a neat dresser. He dressed for the weekly poker game as if he were going to the Berditch-ever Society's annual meeting. He wore a suit with a vest and shoes that were polished like a soldier's. Eva wanted to think he dressed especially for her, but she knew that Malconson dressed for himself. Tessie, who referenced the movies the way other people quoted the Bible, once told her that Mr. Malconson looked like Joseph Cotton. Eva didn't know from Joseph Cotton, but if Tessie said it, then Malconson looked like a movie star.

Molly, Malconson's wife, took no notice of the flirtation, and Harry—well, Harry wouldn't have cared. It was only God Eva worried about. She feared that her desire was tantamount to adultery and that to ask for forgiveness for a sin she intended to repeat only compounded the evil. But it was the spring, and Yom Kippur wasn't until September. Eva, knowing how to turn a deaf ear, even to her own voice, silenced her guilt and continued preparing for the poker game.

The jelly jars and the empty glasses from the memorial candles that served as everyday ware she stowed under the sink. She threw out the tea bags sitting in cups on the counter, even if they'd only been used once. She filled the crystal candy dish with nuts and dates, and she polished the top of the For-mica kitchen table as if it were marble. All this she did with the anticipated pleasure of seeing herself, if only for a few minutes, in the mirror of Malconson's gaze.

Eva heard the doorbell and looked at the clock. It was too early for the poker. Tessie walked into the kitchen with a bouquet of white lilies.

"*Vos iz dos?*" she asked in Yiddish.

"English, Mama," Tessie corrected. "They're flowers."

"So *nu*, I should think they're tomatoes?"

"Mama!"

"They look like the flowers from a goyisher funeral. The Christians do the flowers. They throw them on the graves. If you ask me, it's a waste."

"Ma, these are not from a funeral."

"So, where then?"

"From somebody I met, okay?"

Lately Tessie had become increasingly exasperated with her mother. Eva was different with Tessie. With the other children, she'd rather not see, but with Tessie she was afraid not to look. Tessie had enjoyed being special, but her mother's vigilance had become an impediment to her pleasures. She was getting tired of explaining herself.

Where she was going? What she was wearing? Who she was going with? When was she coming back?

"Ma," she complained, "why are you always asking me and not Ethel or my brothers?"

"*Y* is a crooked letter," Eva said, having learned from Tessie how to defend herself against a good question with a non-answer.

In truth there were three good answers to Tessie's question: one was Eva's guilt, one was unspeakable, and the other was obvious to anyone who saw Tessie. Tessie, with her blonde hair and face like a chiseled cameo, did not look like any other member of Eva's family. Tessie looked like a

Christian, a *shikseh*, and everybody knew about Jewish men and *shiksehs*—they bedded *shiksehs* and married Jews. Tessie looked like she'd been born in Sweden or Norway or one of those blonde countries that Eva would never visit. When Tessie was a baby—and this Eva will never forget—the *yentas* in the neighborhood started a rumor. They stood under her kitchen window and whispered their envy. "She's adopted," they said. "How else would you explain?" they muttered. The rumor started to spread the way milk starts to sour. It made no sense that Eva, already with two mouths to feed, another on the way, and doing piecework in her in-laws' factory, would adopt a baby, but then again when you looked at Tessie, it made no sense that she belonged to Eva.

Tessie grew up hearing the rumors of her adoption. She was secretly pleased. She could imagine herself a Swedish actress—not Greta Garbo, everyone wanted to be Garbo. No, she preferred to think of herself as an actress like Bergman, a little less flash, a little more substance. She valued elegance over glamour. If you asked Tessie how she knew the difference, she couldn't tell you, but truth be told, she got it from Eva.

Even though she looked older than her age, there was elegance about Eva. With her head held high and her spine straight like a pillar, she projected an air of confidence. This she got from her own mother. Eva's mother had told her that when the Cossacks came to the *shtetl*, and the Jews started to run, it was the one that looked weak that got killed first. And so Eva learned that fear can look like confidence, and confidence can look like elegance. To the ladies on Schenck Avenue, confidence looked like arrogance. Eva didn't care— she protected her posture the way a sheep protects a lamb. She never sat on a soft chair. She never dressed without a steel-boned corset. Had Tessie thought to look, she might have seen that it was Eva, not Bergman, who deserved her praise, but, at the moment, all she could see was her own reflection, and all she could hear were her own ruminating thoughts of

Gerry, the guy from the Amboy Dukes, and the flowers in her hand.

"Mama, where's a vase? I need to put these in water or they'll wilt." Eva grudgingly nodded towards the upper cupboard.

"Behind the Passover dishes. There's only one. Be careful. It's all the way in the back. Don't knock the dishes."

"I won't knock them. You think I can't even take down a vase without breaking a dish? You think I can't do anything?"

Eva wasn't sure what Tessie could do. She could look in the mirror—that's what Tessie could do.

As Tessie's exasperation with Eva rose, so did Eva's exasperation with Tessie. Like dough without yeast, Tessie sat on her *toches* and would not get up and get a job. Finally, whether it was Eva's nagging or Tessie's inability to resist anything that had "beauty" in the title, she went to work at Rosa's Beauty Salon around the corner. On Monday morning Tessie got up and put on the pink uniform. On Monday evening she came home wearing a slip. Eva took one look at her daughter and turned her back.

"Why, Ma? What are you looking away? You didn't even hear."

"Yeah, so tell me. Tell me, Tessela. Tell me, where is the uniform?"

Tessie told Eva that Mrs. Hernandez came in, and she had nits. Eva said Tessie had excuses. Eva said you don't quit one job until you have another. Tessie, who loved to star in her own drama, opened her eyes wide, dropped her jaw and shook her head in feigned disbelief.

"I cannot believe . . . I cannot believe that my own mother would want me to wash dirty Puerto Rican heads."

Eva reminded her daughter that Mrs. Hernandez was an immigrant just like her mother.

"You never had nits, Mama!" Tessie said, but Eva wasn't
so sure. When she was fourteen and got off the boat at Ellis
Island, she might have had nits. Her head itched. Her skin
crawled. The guards asked her name, gave her soap and told
her to take a shower. It could be she had nits.

"You want me to get nits, Mama?" Tessie whined.

"I want you should work," Eva countered. "You quit
school. You quit work. So what you gonna do with your time?
You like to dress fancy like a movie star. So who's gonna pay
. . . your father?" And here is where Eva shut her mouth and
bit her tongue in a show of respect for the disrespected. What
was she supposed to tell her daughter? That it was indolence,
not illness, that kept her father home all day?

Tessie, out of respect for her mother, also honored the
family code of silence and did not tell Eva that she was determined not to spend her life wiping noses, washing floors,
and catering to a man who stood at the sink demanding that
his wife get up and get him a glass of water. Besides, Tessie
thought she was already working. In the same way Gerry was
in pursuit of the buck, Tessie was in pursuit of the guy with
the buck. It was a full-time job—clothes, makeup, attitude—it
all took work. If she told this to Eva, Eva would say that her
daughter didn't have to be adopted to be a *shikseh*.

Tessie, tired of arguing with her mother about the job at
Rosa's, decided to enlist her father in her cause. She knew that
Harry, with so few muscles to flex, would grab at the oppor-
tunity to shake a fist at his wife.

Eva was one story, and Harry was another, and together they
were a third. If you looked at their wedding picture, you
would see that Harry was a plain-looking man. Had he been
bad-looking, he would have stood out, but Harry had the mis-
fortune of the nondescript, and unless he was disruptive, he
was unseen. In his wedding picture, he perches on the arm

of a chair in a top hat and tails, his arm loosely around Eva's shoulder. He appears to be looking at nothing. Eva sits in a chair below him. A lace veil crowns her face like a shroud. Her expression is one of resignation. Her eyes look as if she is saying goodbye.

Harry had had a brief interlude of productivity after he married Eva, but then the promise of the future became history, and Harry opted for a premature retirement. Day in and day out, he sat on a hard chair by the window, staring at the brick wall across the alley. He no longer looked like the man Eva married. As he lost substance, he lost weight. Like a tight glove, the skin stretched over the bones of his face, sinking his cheeks and making the hook in his nose all the more prominent. Beaked like an eagle, he could now express his contempt without having to bend his head.

Each morning Harry dressed as if he still had somewhere to go. He put on the slacks to his brown suit and a white shirt with a stiff collar. He hiked up the sleeves with black elastic armbands to protect the cuffs. He buttoned the vest, tucked in the pocket watch, and adjusted the gold chain. Before he left the bedroom, he moved the picture of Eva's parents out of the way to take a last look at himself in the bureau mirror. Harry did not see the character in his face. What Harry saw was what Harry wanted to see—a man who dressed for the office.

Having made the impression on himself that he would like to have made on others, he walked the twenty feet into the kitchen, sat down at the table, and silently waited for Eva to serve him his breakfast.

It irritated Eva to watch Harry eat. He picked at his food like a pigeon pecked at a crumb—a wedge of toast with a little bit of marmalade, sometimes half a bowl of farina—and then he'd sip the coffee through the sugar cube between his teeth. When he was done, he pushed the plate away and left the table. Eva said what a Jewish wife is supposed to say.

"Harry, where you goin'? You eat like a bird. No wonder you don't feel well. Sit down, I'll make you some eggs." Harry brushed her away, turned his back, walked into the living room, and took up his chair.

Harry didn't have to sit on a hard chair. He could have sat on the sofa. It had down cushions. He was thin. He was bony. The sofa would have been easier on his *toches*, but the sofa had flowers, and Harry didn't like flowers. He could have sat in the green armchair, a little frayed but not too bad. It had a standing lamp behind it with a fringe shade and a good bulb. He could have seen to read his paper instead of having to turn it this way and that to catch the light at the window. But there was no talking to Harry. Harry would do whatever he wanted, even if there was nothing he wanted to do. Do not assume he was like Eva. Harry did not choose the hard chair to preserve his posture—his posture, like his stature, was long gone. No, Harry chose the hard chair because for him discomfort was protest, and one way or another, Harry was determined to speak his mind.

While he sat, he smoked Chesterfields. He lit one with the end of another. His fingers, like chicken feet, were yellow from nicotine. He wasn't yet fifty, but he hacked like an old man, and the coughs bent him over. The cigarettes dangled from his lip. Unnoticed, the ash would grow and fall. Small pinholes pocked the carpet in front of Harry's chair. It's hard to say if it was the carpet or the hacking that made Eva crazy, but at least once a day, in broken Yiddish, she would take up her lines and shout into thin air, "You're killing yourself. What the matter with you? Listen to that cough. Meshugha! Smoke and cough. Smoke and cough."

Harry smiled. Eva's litany was proof that he had not lost the capacity to irritate. He'd be damned if he'd stop smoking. Ten years later Eva was right, and Harry was damned. They said it was gallbladder, but Eva knew it was defiance that killed him, and that Harry had spent the last fifteen years sitting his own *shiva*.

Harry's death was a *shandeh*, a shame. He should have walked like a peacock; after all, he was the son of an entrepreneur. This was the selling point Eva's relatives used to get her to say "yes" to his proposal. They didn't think she was getting a bad deal, but it wasn't Eva's happiness they were after, it was a little more space in the tenement apartment. Three rooms, one bathroom down the hall, and eight people. Eva was the last to come, and they thought she should be the first to go, so when Harry proposed and Eva didn't want to budge, they looked at her like she was crazy. Each morning at six before she left for work, and each evening at eight when she came home, her aunt Rifka would start, her uncle Moishe would follow, and her three cousins would echo. Like a chorus they sang, "Oy, Eva, you're gonna argue? What does she expect, the King of England? You're a greenhorn. He's the son of an entrepreneur. Harry Stone is the son of an entrepreneur. Harry Stone is the son of an entrepreneur." Eva, unlike Harry, was unable to protest. She packed her dreams in her suitcase, walked down the aisle and took the oath of servitude.

But why Harry picked Eva is a very good question. Maybe because Sol and Bessie, Harry's parents, sang the same song the other way. They sang, "Oy, Harry what's the matter with you? You're the son of an entrepreneur. Why you gonna marry a greener? What you think, she's the Queen of Sheba? You're the son of an entrepreneur. You're the son of an entrepreneur."

For Harry, whatever Sol and Bessie didn't want was the very least that he could do. He went to Goldstein, the jeweler, picked out a ring—not too big, not too small—Eva stuck out her finger, Harry slid it on, and that was that.

The Stone & Sons dry goods store, a hole in the wall on the corner of Schenck and New Lots, became a two-thousand-foot shop on Pitkin and then a five-thousand-foot factory downtown on Atlantic Avenue. When Harry's older brother,

Morris, left the business to work for Bulova Watch in New York City, Sol dropped *& Sons*, and the name became Stone Lingerie. Harry began to worry whether he was being phased out of the business. Harry wanted to sit where his father sat—in an office, in a suit, by a phone, with a desk. Harry hated being on the dirty floor, listening all day to the clacking of the sewing machines. He wanted to come home clean instead of covered in lint. When Harry asked his father how come he didn't just take off the *s* and leave the *Son*, Sol raised himself to his full five-feet-two height, balanced on his toes, and shouted, "What you care what we call it? Your brother quit, so someday I'll retire, and he'll get nothin', and you'll get everything. Your job is to make sure every pair of bloomers, every slip that leaves this factory, is worth my name. That's your job. You hear me, Harry? That's your job."

Harry heard, but he didn't answer. What was he going to say to his father: *I want you should be dead so I can sit in your chair?* He went back on the floor and watched the girls—making sure they sewed the seams straight, put the darts where the pattern showed, and didn't skimp on the lace. Like a Jew prays for the Messiah, Harry prayed for the "someday."

"Someday" never came. Sol never left. Maybe he kept waiting for the prodigal son to quit Bulova and come back where he belonged. But when Harry realized that Sol had no plans to retire, Harry got sick so he could get out. He came home one Friday night, sat down at the table, sipped a little soup with a matzah ball, and said he couldn't swallow it anymore. Eva tried to get him to take some mineral oil. Harry pushed it away and told Eva to pour him some schnapps. Eva said the whiskey would burn. Harry told her to pour the schnapps. The next morning, he got up, took a chair from the kitchen, put it by the living room window, sat down, and waited fifteen years to digest what he couldn't swallow.

Tessie stood in front of her father and waited for the smoke to clear so she could get his attention. When she told Harry about Rosa's, she watched her father's indignation rise like a flush. He went running into the kitchen and in broken Yiddish he yelled at his wife. "No daughter of mine is going to wash the head of a dirty spic. What's the matter with you? You crazy? You *meshuganah*?"

Eva shut her ears and calmed herself with thoughts of Malconson. Harry, satisfied that he had made his point, went back to his chair in the living room. Tessie left Eva in the kitchen and went into her bedroom, avoiding her sister Ethel and her annoying questions. She needed to pick out an outfit, hoping for a date with Gerry.

Pauline and Louis

when they were eight

Gerry took Tessie to Enrico's to impress her. The linen tablecloths and the china dishes, he thought, would make the evening.

"Should I call you George or Gerry?" Tessie asked.

"Gerry! Except to my sister, I'm not George no more. There's a story about me and my sister, but it's too long.

"We've got time, right? Tell your story."

Tessie shook out her napkin, classy-like, and laid it in her lap.

Back in 1926, the year his father Louie died, his mother Pauline had an apartment on Linden Boulevard on the fourth floor of a six-floor building. It was a railroad flat. Rooms jutted off a long, narrow hall like legs off a centipede. The floors in the building had white mosaic tiles with a black, Greek-key border, an attempt at elegance by the builders but unappreciated by the tenants. Who could see the floors? The stairs were narrow and the landings crowded. Pauline kept telling her friend Gertie to take the baby carriage off the landing.

She was going to break her neck going up and down these God-damned steps. Gertie said Pauline should come into her apartment and tell her where to put it. Pauline wanted to tell her where to put it, but Louie told her to be nice, so Pauline just gave Gertie a look and kept climbing.

The building next door also had six floors. From her apartment, Pauline could look up and see the window from which her sister Sarah had taken a leap, or she could look down and see where Louie had dropped in his tracks. If she looked across the street, she saw the Catholic orphanage where she'd threatened to put George since the day Louie died. George wished he didn't believe her, but he did. He saw it by the way she didn't look at him. His sister Laura told him not to cry. It was just that he looked so much like his father that when their mother looked at him, her heart broke even more. George didn't know how to feel about that; if it was good or if it was bad. He looked across the street. The nuns in their habits looked like bats. George tried to stay out of sight. He didn't want to remind his mother of what she didn't want to remember, but when "one more mouth to feed" became his middle name, he stopped running home and started running away.

The picture of Pauline was taken a few months after Louie died. She is wearing a white shirt, maybe silk, open at the collar. Her wedding band hangs on a thin, gold chain around her neck. Her elbow rests on a table, and one finger touches her cheek, giving her a look of poise and puzzlement. Her thick, dark hair is pulled back from her face. She is an artist's sketch with her high cheekbones, perfect nose, and sensuous mouth, but grief has frozen her expression and taken the light out of her eyes, and the picture has no depth.

Who knew why Louie died? He was thirty-four, the picture of health. It was a hernia, a simple operation, nothing. The doctor said he could do it in his sleep. Pauline wonders if maybe he did. Why else would her Louie walk out of the hospital one day and drop dead the next? Kaplan, Sarah's husband, stricken and angry for his own inexplicable loss, said that Louie was an idiot; who goes bowling right after a surgery? Pauline told Kaplan he's *meshugah*, that's why her sister jumped out the window. Who could live with such a *meshuganah*? For the hundredth time she explained to her brother-in-law that Louie had not gone bowling; he'd gone around the corner like always to Al's bar for a *bisel* schnapps. She'd asked Al. Al said that Louie was fine. He drank his drink. He walked out the door. He turned the corner and dropped like a stone.

If you asked the yentas in the neighborhood, they'd tell you it was Pauline. They'd say that Louie was not a *schlemiel*; he knew to stay in bed after an operation. They'd say that Louie went to Al's to get away from Pauline. They'd say Pauline was a beauty without a heart, and Louie was a devil with a wandering eye.

George, eight years old, trying to make sense out of no sense, would tell you that his father died because his mother was right: he was a "no-good kid." Why else would his father leave him? They'd had big plans. They were going to go fishing in Sheepshead Bay. They were going to go to Ebbets Field to see the Dodgers beat the Giants. They were going to go to the playground after dinner and pitch a few, and now nothing but nothing. That's what George would've told you then; now, at twenty-two, having learned to take the blame for nothing and to never admit to anything, he would tell you whatever it was you wanted to hear.

The morning of the day Louie died, George got up and dressed for school. He put on his shirt with his knickers. He wanted long pants. He told his father that all the boys in third grade had long pants already. Louie, advocating for his son, suggested to his wife that maybe it was time. Pauline told Louie that the last time she'd put George in long pants, he'd

played in the vacant lot, fallen in the dirt, ripped the knees—
and that was the end of the long pants.

"Your son thinks you're a prince and not a painter. Tell
him that money doesn't grow on trees. Tell him how many
hours you have to paint Mrs. Schmidt's apartment to buy him
one thing after another."

Louie looked at George and gave him a hug and a kiss
and whispered loud enough for Pauline to hear, that soon,
the two of them would take a walk over to Pitkin Avenue to
the haberdashery so George could pick out a new pair of long
pants. George gave his father a hug, Pauline gave Louie a
smile, secretly happy that Louie could give George the love
that she couldn't muster for a son she didn't want.

Pauline remembered how, in the second month when the
blood didn't come, she'd begun to pull her hair out. Her Louie
already worked till all hours to pay the rent and buy the food.
She already had a beautiful child, her daughter Laura. Gertie
said Pauline should go to shul and ask God for help. Pauline
told Gertie she'd sooner ask a gangster for a loan. As far as
Pauline was concerned, God was in it for himself. If Gertie
didn't believe her, she should have been on the deck of the boat
coming over and seen how two mothers with dead babies had
climbed out of steerage, gone to the rail, and dropped their
hearts into the sea.

"God," she told Gertie, "didn't lift a finger. If you ask me,
God makes you miserable so you should go to shul, rock back
and forth like an idiot, bend at the knee, and ask him for forgiveness. God collects prayers the way the mob collects money,
so he can sit on his ass like a *macher*. If God was less interested
in being a big shot and more interested in helping a Jew, he'd
get off his *toches* and make life a little easier for my Louie."

Gertie shook her head and smiled at Pauline. "You wait;
when the third month comes and still no blood, you'll go to
shul." The third month came. Pauline didn't go to God; she
went next door to her sister Sarah.

Pauline climbed the steps to the sixth floor and walked into her sister's apartment. Sarah was sitting the way she always sat: in a housedress, with a net over her hair, stockings rolled down around her ankles, humming a Russian song. Sarah remembered the tune, but the words were lost. Pauline looked around the kitchen and felt her sister's despair. The dishes from last night, from this morning, were piled in the sink. The pots, with a soup—maybe lentil, maybe chicken, who could tell?—sat on the stove. After Ruthie was born, Sarah was okay; it was when Herbie came that Sarah fell apart.

Pauline grabbed a chair and sat knee to knee, trying to make Sarah look at her. She took both of her sister's hands and held them in her lap.

"Sarah," she whispered, "stop the humming. Look at me. I have a problem, Sarah. Maybe you can help?"

Sarah came out of her reverie and looked at her sister. "What? What, Pauline? Is it Mama?"

"No. Sarah. You forget? Mama died before we took the boat."

"Oh," Sarah nodded, remembering again. "Oy! Mama," she began to whimper.

"No, Sarahala don't cry. Mama's good where she is. Mama is smiling. Mama is happy," Pauline said, comforting her.

Sarah, reassured, glanced up and looked at her sister. "So what, Pauline?"

"Sarah," Pauline asked, "after Ruthie, after Herbie, there was another, yes?" Sarah nodded. "So, what happened? Where did it go?"

"It went."

"Yes, but how?"

"The piano."

"What, Sarah? You're talking crazy. What're you talking, the piano?"

"The piano," Sarah reiterated. "I jumped off the piano, the blood came, and that was that. *Shoyn*. Finished. Done."

What Pauline never got around to telling Louie, she kept telling George: how she should have listened to her sister and jumped off the piano. Five years later, when Sarah took the leap, Pauline wondered if maybe Sarah had been pregnant again, but that this time the piano didn't work.

George tightened the leather strap around his books, gave his mother a quick peck on the cheek, and tried not to run over his sister going out the door. Already late, he took the shortcut through the lot. The lot was an eyesore in the neighborhood. Everything that used to be something had been dumped in the lot. The debris of local life was strewn over the square block of dirt and sand: broken radiators and pipes, prams without wheels, rags that used to be clothes. On hot days the garbage stank in the sun, and on wet days it floated in the mud.

Like most kids, George went where he wasn't supposed to go. He scavenged the rubble for toys and treasures. He found two pennies and a condom. He pocketed the pennies but could find no use for a broken balloon. He figured by now he was late, so he ran like crazy until his foot caught in some wire and he fell on his back. When he picked himself up he saw that the back pocket of his pants had a small rip. He tried to pinch it together with his fingers. He knew if his mother saw, it was the end of the long pants.

When he got across the lot, he ran the two blocks to school. It was five minutes before the bell. The kids were still running around the yard. He saw little Eddie and Manny and coaxed them into a fast game of Johnny-on-the pony. George was a wiry, scrappy kid. Maybe he weighed sixty, seventy pounds at the most. It's not that he didn't eat—he ate everything in sight, but he burned it up like kindling. Pauline would tell you she couldn't put meat on his bones. The yentas would think she didn't feed him.

Manny bent over, put his head against the wall, and

braced himself for the first jumper. The kids, one on top of the other, took the leap and mounted Manny. George was the last to jump on. He walked back, took a running start and leapt like a tiger. It would have been good except that Iggy, the kid in the middle, couldn't hang on, and the whole pile went down on top of George. When he got up and brushed himself off, the small rip had become a big tear, and he knew that was that for the long pants. He felt guilty, not for the pants, but for his father. His father had stood up for him, and George had let him down. What could Louie say to Pauline now?

George dragged his feet walking home. He was in no hurry to face the music. When he entered his building, he knew something wasn't right. There was a loud, screeching sound ricocheting off the wall. George wanted to turn and run, but he kept climbing the steps. When he got to his landing, he saw people spilling out of his apartment. He wove his way through the crowd towards the eerie sound. No one seemed to see him. When he walked into the dining room, he saw his father lying on his back on the table and realized that the eerie sound was coming out of his mother's throat.

His sister Laura saw him. She came over and put her arm around his shoulder and pulled him close. Laura was only eleven months older than George, but he trusted her more than anything, because everything she said was true.

"Daddy is dead," she whispered. George looked at his father, eyes closed, skin gray like a fish, and he felt warm pee run down his leg. He rushed from the room and hid under the bed. Later, after only a few people were left—his uncle Kaplan, Gertie from downstairs, and his cousins Herbie and Ruthie—Laura coaxed him out from under the bed. His clothes were stuck to him, and he smelled like the bathroom in the basement at school. Laura told him to undress and put him in a bath. When he was done and all cleaned up, she combed his hair and told him to go into the dining room and give his mother a kiss. He wanted to tell his mother about the pants and tell her that it was okay if she didn't want to buy him another pair. He approached her on tiptoes, trying not to look at his father on the table. Pauline picked her head up off Louie's body and looked at her son but saw nothing.

Later that night, the undertaker came, covered Louie's body with a cloth, put him on a cart, and tried to wheel him out the door. George and Laura peeked out from the bedroom. They saw their mother holding on to the cart as if it were a lifeboat in the sea. Kaplan was begging Pauline to let go. Finally, he grabbed her waist from behind and pulled while the undertakers pried her fingers loose. Louie left on the cart, the door slammed, and Pauline collapsed in a heap. Laura ran out from the bedroom and lay down beside her mother. Pauline put her arm around her daughter and held her like a teddy bear.

George, tears streaming down his face, circled his mother and his sister, trying to find a place to fit in, but they were tight like a fist. He gave up, walked out of the hall, and went into his parents' bedroom. He opened the door to Louie's closet where he found the humidor with the tobacco. He found the pipe Louie smoked, the one he'd put under George's nose, laughing and telling him to take a whiff. He pulled a pair of Louie's pants off the hanger, put them on over his pajamas, and shuffled to his room. He climbed into Laura's bed and waited for her to come in and lie down beside him.

The next day they walked behind the hearse in Beth David Cemetery. It was cold. The wind was blowing. Icy pellets hung on the trees like stalactites. Laura held him close to keep him warm and to warm herself. Pauline, already frozen, was impervious to the cold. She wore a black dress with a high collar. Her coat was unbuttoned, and it flapped in the wind like the wings of a hawk. George dropped Laura's hand and ran up to his mother. He took her hand between his palms and touched it to his cheek. It was icy cold. He did what his father would have done. He rubbed it and kissed it. Pauline seemed unaware. When George let go, her arm snapped to her side like a limb off a dead tree. George knew his father was in the coffin, but he'd no idea where his mother had gone. He left her side and went back to walk with his sister.

George watched as they lowered his father into the ground. He looked at Pauline and saw his mother's eyes widen in horror as each shovelful of earth hit the casket. The rabbi turned to George, as the man of the house, and asked him if he wanted to take his turn. George left Laura, walked up to the grave, and with both hands lifted the shovel. It was too heavy for a little boy, and it teetered as he tried to bring the earth to the grave. George heard the hollow clump as the dirt hit the coffin. He believed then, if he hadn't before, that he'd had a hand in burying his father. He dropped the shovel and ran to Pauline, wrapping his arms around her legs. She lifted her arms; they hovered over his shoulders, a wish for a gesture she could not make. The chill wind blew, and George ran back to Laura to keep warm.

They were up to dessert when Gerry finished his story. He ordered for them both—two cheesecakes. Tessie liked that Gerry took charge. Gerry liked that Tessie was a good listener. Gerry wondered if he should have left out the part about peeing his pants? Nah, he thought, what the hell, he was only eight.

When the meal was over and they got in the car, he pulled her to him and gave her a deep, long kiss. She was hot, so he took liberties and reached his hand into her pants. His finger traced a deep scar.

"What's this?" he asked.

"*That's* a story," she said.

"Well tell me," he said, knowing that she would be flattered by his interest. "I showed you mine; now you show me yours," he said with a laugh.

She leaned back on the seat and lit a cigarette.

"Okay," she said, and she began where it started, way back in 1926.

Her Grandfather Sol had miscalculated. The ladies weren't buying the bloomers. He couldn't understand—how could they stop wearing bloomers? Who knew with women? He asked his wife Bessie if she still wore bloomers.

"What? You want to know if I wear bloomers? Maybe if you came home and went to the bed the way you get up and go to the factory, you'd know if I wear bloomers."

"Yeah, Bessie." Sol was disgusted hearing the same old complaint. "I won't go to the factory. I'll stay home. You go to work; you make the money."

Bessie went back to whatever it was she was doing. There was no point in arguing with Sol. There was never any point in arguing with Sol.

Sol kept puzzling. How could they go without bloomers? He made a good garment. It made no sense. Never willing to take no for an answer, he figured any day there'd be a rush to buy, so he began to make more when he should have made less. Sol was running after his own tail. The girls in the factory got irritated. Sol was cutting salaries, laying off workers but demanding more output. Finally, it dawned on Sol what was going on. The mobsters had begun to infiltrate the shop and agitate the girls. The word "union" became a familiar sound. The wise guys made a visit. They told Sol that for a small donation, they'd quiet the girls and make sure the ladies were wearing Sol's bloomers. Sol gave them what for and told them to get the hell out of his shop. Bessie, alarmed, said that maybe Sol should be a little more charitable.

"What are you, *meshugah*? You give those lousy good-for-nothings a dime, and they'll want a dollar.

As his blood pressure went up, his pitch began to rise. He banged his fist on the table.

"Nobody, you hear Bessie, *nobody* sucks the blood out of Sol Stone. They want money from Sol, they can come to work. I'll give them a job. They can pack the boxes, sweep the floor, kiss my ass. You hear me, Bessie? Not one dime do they get from Sol Stone."

Sol, trying not to agitate the girls—they shouldn't say he played favorites—laid Eva off. When Eva asked Sol how she was supposed to feed his grandchildren with no job, Sol told her to tell his son to get off his ass and go to work. Eva came home in a panic. She asked Harry to talk to his father. Harry, happier for Sol's troubles than he was worried for his own, told Eva there was no point in talking to deaf ears, and maybe his wife should stop making brisket and start making chicken. Eva told Harry that the difference between here and the poor house wasn't a brisket. Harry went back to his chair, and Eva went to Heshy's Bakery and took a job delivering.

At five in the morning, Eva would get up. In the dark, before the heat came up in the radiator, she would step onto the cold linoleum, quietly tiptoe to the bathroom, get dressed, put on her blue wool coat, and go the ten blocks to Heshy's. She was happy that it was still dark; the yentas shouldn't see her. At Heshy's it was warm. The bakers had been up since four, and the ovens were going. The bread, the challah, and the bagels, golden brown, were already coming out of the ovens. The smells reminded her of the smells in the *shtetl* on Friday morning when the women were getting ready for the Sabbath.

Heshy would tell Eva to sit and give her a little coffee to sip. He would break off the twist on top of challah; she should have a little bite before she went out in the cold. He would fill the basket for the first run.

Eva had a route. She'd walk down Schenck and up Livonia. Lights were coming on, and she would knock on doors to see who would want a challah, some bagels, or maybe some bialys. As she walked and as they bought, the load got lighter. When the basket was empty, she would go back to Heshy's to fill it, and she'd go out again. Heshy paid her by the loaf, so Eva ran to make as much as she could in the time that she had. By seven, she was done. Heshy would fold the money, push it into her pocket, and give her a loaf to take home. She would hurry back to the children. Get them up, feed them breakfast, and get them off to school. Afterwards, when the house got quiet, she would wait and pray that Sol would get an order and send one of the girls over to tell her he needed her in the shop. In the meantime, she began to make aprons and housedresses and anything else she could think of to sell to the peddlers, to sell to the yentas.

The days when one or the other of the children got sick, which in winter was every other day, Eva did what she had to do. She put her hand on the forehead or her ear to the chest and told them yes they could stay in bed, or no they should get up and go to school. If their head was hot, she told them to run the water, not too hot and not too cold, and take a bath. If the air rattled in their lungs, she ran quick and made a mustard plaster, put it on their chest, and told them to stay in bed, and if their nose was stuffed and they couldn't breathe, she took them into the kitchen, put a towel over their heads, and told them to lean over the steaming kettle.

The day that Tessie got sick and cried that her stomach hurt, Eva gave her some mineral oil and told her to get up and get dressed and go to school. Tessie wouldn't budge. She said it hurt too much. Eva, having finally gotten a call from Sol, gave in to Tessie and told her to do whatever she wanted to do. She was eight years old, she wasn't a baby, and if she wanted to stay home and lie around like a noodle, she should stay. Before Eva left to go to Sol's, she yelled to Harry to keep an eye on their daughter.

"Sure, sure," he said, brushing her off, angry that she worried more for the kids than she did for him. Harry did what Harry did; he sat and waited for Eva to come home and make his lunch, and then he sat and waited for Eva to come home and make his dinner.

Later that evening, Eva walked in the house and went in to check on Tessie. She was whimpering. Eva sat down on the bed and rubbed her belly and kissed her forehead and asked if maybe she would like a little soup.

"I'll heat up a little chicken soup. I'll put in a little chicken, some carrots. It will be good. You should eat a little something."

Tessie refused. She turned away from Eva, pulled her legs up to her chest and lay like an infant in the corner of the bed. What was Eva going to do? She kissed her forehead and hoped that when she awoke tomorrow, the fever would be gone and Tessie would be better.

The next day when Eva came home, Tessie was crying, and the next day when Eva came home, Tessie was screaming. Eva heard the screams even before she got to the steps. Rachel and Libby, the yentas next door, were standing at the stoop waiting for Eva.

"Your daughter has been screaming all day. Where were you? Your daughter is sick. You should take her to the doctor."

Eva pushed past them in a rush to get to Tessie. She tried to hide her shame and appear impervious. Eva's air was like oxygen to a fire, and the yentas shook their heads in disbelief. Eva heard Rachel tell Libby that if Eva's neglect weren't going to kill one child, it would kill another. Eva thought that this one's husband was working and that one's husband was working. They could go to a doctor, open their purse, and pay him his fee, but what was Eva going to pay a doctor—a challah, a chicken?

When Eva opened the door, Harry was standing by the bedroom door, hands up, not knowing what to do. Eva leaned down beside her child.

"Tessela? Tessela?" she whispered. She put her lips to Tessie's forehead and it was as if she were kissing the oven.

"Oy, my gut! Oy, my gut!" Eva pulled Tessie up and held her to her bosom and rocked her and held her, but Tessie was limp. Eva yelled to Harry, "Why didn't you call me?" She threw up her hands. "Call now, Harry, call now!"

"Call who, Eva? Who do you want me to call?"

Eva shook her head at Harry and ran to the corner to the candy store and asked Francis if she could use the phone. She called an ambulance. "Please, please come. *Mein dauchter* is dying. Please," she begged.

"Please," she cried. "*Mein dauchter.* Mein Tessie. I'm sorry. I'm sorry."

The ambulance came. Tessie went to the hospital. Her appendix had burst and peritonitis set in. Her fever raged. The doctor told Eva to go home. He did what he could do. There was no point. She would live. She would die. It was God's choice, not his. Eva was frightened that if she left Tessie now the way she'd left her before, God would punish her neglect by taking her daughter. She ran home only for an hour, made the supper, came back and sat. The next day, she ran home, made the supper, came back and sat. For eight days Eva ran home, made the supper, came back, and sat. On the ninth day, Tessie was released from the hospital, thin like a bone. Her little cheeks were gone, and her face was sunken. Her skin was sallow, but she was alive.

Trauma, like hot heat, warps memory into strange shapes. The real and the unreal become apparitions of what was and what wasn't. Like George when he lost his father, Tessie only remembers fragments of those days, moments stamped in memory like pictures taken with a flash. She remembers smells and sounds. She remembers the pain that twisted her body into a scream. As in a haze, she thinks she remembers her sister Ethel kneeling next to her bed and whispering, promising something if only she wouldn't . . . but Tessie can't remember what it was she shouldn't . . . Was her brother Izzy there? She thinks she remembers Izzy telling her not to cry. Telling her that Mama was coming and not to cry. She remembers her tongue was dry like sand, but water made her wretch. She remembers being hot and cold and hot. She thinks she remembers being put on a stretcher and carried down the stairs and put in a truck. Is this a memory, or a fantasy that became a reality? She's not sure. How can she know? She was very, very sick. She was only eight years old. She was alone, and it was dark. She would have asked her mother to tell her what happened, but she thinks she remembers that her mother wasn't there.

When the story was all out of her, finished, Tessie sighed and turned away from Gerry.

"What's the matter?" he asked.

"I don't know. It feels funny hearing it out loud."

"Nah, don't," he said. "It's an important story."

Gerry wondered if her story was better than his. He'd told her the truth, as it happened, but, because it hadn't conveyed the impression he wanted to make, Gerry decided to make it better. He told Tessie how back when his father died, he sat by his mother all night, stroking her back. He told Tessie how grateful his mother was to have a loving son to take care of her.

Tessie liked this story. The image of Gerry as a caretaker was the one she wanted to have. Gerry liked it too, and so he kept it, until the lie became the truth.

When they were both finished talking, Gerry tried to turn her on again, but the moment was lost. It didn't matter, because Tessie was determined to play hard to get. She wasn't going to be like her sister Ethel and give it away for free.

∽ negative space ∾

E thel was sitting at the vanity, applying the bright coral lipstick she'd bought especially to match her bright coral blouse. Tessie stood at the doorway, observing. She saw how Ethel's ass hung over the back of the bench and how her large breasts pushed against the buttons of her blouse. Tessie thought, with satisfaction, that Ethel was about ten pounds past voluptuous.

"You're doing it wrong," Tessie said.

Ethel grimaced in the mirror.

"What? What am I doing wrong?"

"The lipstick. You're trying to make a Clara Bow mouth. You don't have a Clara Bow mouth. You have a Harry Stone mouth. *Dad's* mouth. You have to work with what you've got."

"Yeah? Says who?" asked Ethel.

"If you don't want my help, fine. If you want to look like a floozy, what do I care?"

Ethel wished she could tell Tessie to take a hike, but she knew that Tessie knew what looked good. Tessie was thin. She had style. She wore wide-leg slacks and spectator shoes. Ethel swallowed her pride and asked Tessie to show her.

"Look at me," Tessie said, taking the lipstick. She carefully traced Ethel's lips. "It's like when you color, you try to stay in the lines."

When Tessie was done, and Ethel looked in the mirror, she saw what she didn't want to see, her father's face—small dark eyes, beaked nose, thin lips, and weak chin. Ethel knew she was no looker. She tried to make up in personality what she lacked in looks. She was what guys called *fun-loving*.

Tessie looked at her sister. "Much better," she said. "Izzy and Seymour are here. Go show your brothers; they'll tell you, too."

Tessie and Izzy and Seymour were like a queen and two kings. They made it clear that Ethel didn't belong in their royal court. They offered her no friendship and no solace, but Ethel knew she served a purpose. She was the negative space—without her they'd have trouble defining themselves. There was only one person in the family Ethel trusted, and that was their oldest brother, Hymie. Nobody else in the family liked Hymie either. Ethel and Hymie were like the peasants outside the palace—they shared what they had, and on cold nights, they kept each other warm.

When Tessie left the bedroom, Ethel stood up from the vanity, shimmied her skirt down over her hips, licked her fingers, and straightened the seams of her stockings. She reached for the key hidden behind the mahogany bureau. On the bureau stood a small curio cabinet. Inside the cabinet were the twelve glass animals that Hymie had given her over the years—the first, the elephant, he gave her when she was five years old. She later found out he had filched it from a tourist shop on 42nd street. She didn't care. It was special and just for her. The rest he said he'd bought with money he earned, but he never said how he earned the money.

She was late. Her friend Chicky was waiting; there was no time to do what she liked to do—what she'd done since she was a child—run the glass animals up her arms and along her legs. On nights when Tessie was out, and she had the bedroom to herself, she would choose one animal to be special and put it between her legs until the heat of her body warmed the cool of the glass. Soothed, she would carefully return it to the cabinet, lock it, and hide the key, but tonight there was no time. She blew them kisses, grabbed a shrug from Tessie's drawer, and ran out of the house.

Ethel worked as a secretary at the Brooklyn Navy Yard. It was 1941. America was about to enter the war, and the yard was alive with anticipation and apprehension. It was a schlep from home, two trolleys, but Ethel didn't mind. She was excited to be part of something important, and it didn't hurt that there were guys everywhere.

It was that night that she met Eddie—a double date with Chicky and Albert. Chicky said that Eddie was Albert's best friend. She promised Ethel that he was a swell guy.

"And what are you worried about?" she asked Ethel, "It's not like you've been so particular lately."

Ethel laughed. Chicky had her number. They'd been friends since first grade.

"Well you're not exactly the Virgin Mary," Ethel said.

Chicky was right about Eddie; he was a swell guy. He was tall and well-built with dark hair. He had a sallow complexion like a faded suntan but nice warm eyes. He was a *shaigitz*, a Christian. Ethel didn't care. What mattered to her was that he was 4F. He wasn't going anywhere anytime soon. Chicky said not to mention the 4F, as Eddie was a little sensitive in that area. She said that he had a breathing problem—asthma, she thought.

"Don't worry. I'm not saying nothin'. Why would I embarrass the guy? Geez, Chicky. Do you think I'm an idiot?" Ethel asked.

"Just sayin'," said Chicky.

In deference to Eddie, they decided not to go see Gary Cooper in *Sergeant York*, even though Chicky thought Gary Cooper was the cat's meow. Instead they opted for Bogart and Mary Astor in *The Maltese Falcon*. It was the right choice because after, when they went out for a couple of drinks, Eddie couldn't stop talking about Bogart's Sam Spade, and Ethel couldn't stop talking about Mary Astor's dress.

Ethel and Eddie hit it off well enough for a couple of months, but then Eddie got bored and moved on. For a while, Ethel called it quits and stayed at home with her glass animals. She really liked Eddie, but soon she started dating Marvin. Marvin was okay, but he was no Eddie, and when Ethel realized she was pregnant, she ignored Marvin and decided it must have been Eddie's kid.

Eddie said he'd come up with the lettuce so she could get rid of it. Ethel didn't want an abortion; she wanted Eddie. She went to her father, confessed that she was pregnant, confessed that Eddie was a *shagitz*. She begged her father to have some *rachmones*, empathy for his youngest child, and give them money for a wedding.

Harry was disgusted with Ethel.

"Enough, already," he shouted in Yiddish. "*Gai avek*, go away," he cried. "A wedding—you want a wedding? And who's going to marry you and a *shagitz*, a priest?"

Ethel begged Tessie to talk to Harry on her behalf.

"He'll listen to you," she said. "He always listens to you."

Tessie took pity on her sister. She also wanted the bedroom to herself. She went and spoke to their father.

The next day Harry got off his chair, went to his brother Moishe and borrowed five thousand dollars. Moishe kissed the money goodbye. He knew he'd never see a dime from Harry but he did what brothers do, one for the other. When he came home, he went into the bedroom and found Ethel playing with her glass animals. He threw the animals on the floor and the money on the bed.

"*Gai avek*. Go away, you're a *shandeh*," he yelled in Yiddish.

Ethel, shaken, picked the slivers out of the hem of the pink chenille bedspread, where they'd attached themselves.

The larger shards on the floor she placed back in the curio cabinet. Then, with bloodied fingers, she counted out the money her father had thrown—$5000. When she stuffed the money under the pillow and felt the intact body of the elephant, her tears broke and she sobbed.

The next day she handed the money to Eddie and made a half-hearted joke that it was blood money—a week later they eloped. Three weeks later, Ethel miscarried. Although 4F, Eddie felt as if he had been given an honorable discharge. He asked Ethel to leave, so she packed her bag and went home.

"Where's the money?" Harry asked.

Ethel said there was no money. "Eddie took the money."

Harry threw up his hands. "You're no daughter of mine," he said.

Ethel sat at the vanity and looked in the mirror. Her face was swollen. Her eyes were bloodshot. She called Hymie, but he wasn't home, so she soothed herself with the elephant—ran him up her arms, held him against her cheeks, and then, with slow, careful strokes, she took the coral lipstick and painted on a Clara Bow mouth.

putting the pieces together

It is September 1947, and we are moving to Redfield Village in Metuchen, New Jersey. Redfield Village is what you would call garden apartments: two-story, red brick buildings and large manicured lawns that angle around cul-de-sacs.

My mother, in a very no-nonsense voice, tells my father and me that she doesn't want to move. She says that she belongs in Brooklyn near her mother and her siblings and the *gantseh meshpokha*, the whole family. To move away is a slap in the face to all of them. She tells him the only reason she is going is because he hasn't been coming home at night, and she knows it's not just because the factory is a schlep, although she agrees that driving an hour and forty-five minutes from Perth Amboy, New Jersey, back to Brooklyn at the end of a long day is a pain in the ass. But the real reason she is moving is because she'll be damned if she is going to sit around, waiting for him to come home while he is *fooling around* with Lillian the secretary.

"I'm not an idiot," she tells him. "You think I don't know what you're up to?"

Whenever my mother brings up Lillian the secretary, my father tells her she is crazy and doesn't know what she's talking about.

My father manufactures ladies' handbags. Inside a big, gray, cement building, ladies sit at sewing machines with extra big needles. The whole building smells of musky leather. There are rows and rows of wooden trays balanced on wooden sawhorses. Blue, red, and green handbags—some with snaps and some with wooden handles—stick up on the trays like crayons in my Crayola box. The name of the factory is Terose Leather: Fine Handbags for Fine Ladies. He tells my mother that the *Te* in Terose is for the first two letters of her name, Tessie, but he won't tell her who the *ro* and *se* are for. He says he just made them up because it sounded good, but my mother doesn't believe him. At least there is no *li*, so he didn't name it after Lillian—or me, for that matter.

My mother doesn't believe a lot of things my father says, because *he promises but he doesn't deliver.* When I get disappointed, she tells me that if I'd listened to her and waited for him to put his money where his mouth is, I wouldn't always be disappointed. My father says that my mother has no faith.

I'm thinking that my father is right, and maybe if my mother had faith, he would *want* to come home for dinner. So when he sits down on my bed to kiss me goodnight and tells me that he is super sorry but he was super busy and didn't have time to get the circus tickets, and promises me that next year we will *absolutely, definitely* go to the Ringling—I believe him. I have faith in him. When he says that as soon as the factory takes off, he will buy us a real house like the one his sister, Aunt Laura, has in Franklin Square, my mother says, "Yeah. Well I'm from Missouri—*show me.*" But I believe him.

After we move to Redfield, we go to Grandma's house every Saturday and to Aunt Laura and Uncle Harry's house every Sunday. Aunt Laura is always happy to see us and especially her brother. Aunt Laura is only eleven months older than my father, but when Grandpa Louie died and my grandma Pauline *lost it*, my aunt Laura had to take care of her little brother. So she always seems much older. She had to be like his mom.

Aunt Laura treats my father like a king. She makes him his favorite—eggplant. Uncle Harry sits in his chair, smokes his pipe, and doesn't even look up when we come in. He says Aunt Laura bends over backwards for her brother. He says that she doesn't bend over any which way for him, and then he laughs. I don't see what's so funny about bending over, backwards or forwards. "He hates us," my mother says to my father. "Your brother-in-law can't stand us. He treats us like we're *shmattehs*, and still you want to go there every week."

"She's my sister," is all my father answers. The way he says it makes me wish I had a sister to feel that way about, but my mother only had one child. "Believe me, you were enough!" she tells me, over and over.

But I do have my cousin Louise, who says that her father is angry because we come over all the time, and because her mother always sticks up for her brother, even if he is a jerk.

"My father is not a jerk," I protest.

"My father says he is."

"Well maybe a little, sometimes," I say.

I tell my mother after we leave that she's prettier than Aunt Laura—particularly when she smiles—and this is true. In her wedding picture, she is beautiful.

Aunt Laura collects little shoes made out of colored glass and white porcelain. She keeps them in a glass cabinet so they are protected from dust and also from my cousin Alan, a bratty little kid who roughhouses in the living room. At Aunt Laura's house, we eat in the dining room on a tablecloth with silver candlesticks. Uncle Harry hands his plate to Aunt Laura and she fills it first because he is the boss of the house. My father says that my mother should take a few lessons from his sister. My mother says, "Over my dead body."

Aunt Laura is happy and smiles a lot. My mother says she has lots to smile about; she has a real house with furniture and a backyard and a barbecue and a piano, and a husband who comes home at night.

My cousin Louise is six months younger than I am. We are close like sisters, but we do not look alike. I'm a skinny minny. I have thick, brown, wavy hair that my mother puts in pigtails. When we are going to Aunt Laura's, she adds ribbons to hide the rubber bands. I have long legs and bony knees with red scabs, because I am learning to ride a two-wheeler. Louise has light brown, frizzy hair that she hates. She is a little on the fat side. Once we heard our mothers say that I'm the pretty one and Louise is the smart one. I don't think that's fair. Sometimes I'm smart, and sometimes Louise is pretty. You don't have to be everything all the time. But when our mothers take us shopping together and we have to take Louise to Bonwit Tellers, because that's the store that has the chubby shop, I am secretly glad. Louise hates going there. She makes Aunt Laura wait out in the store and won't let her into the fitting room. In the stores where we're shopping for me, I parade everything I try on. By the time we go to lunch, she's so angry, she ends up eating everything: meatloaf, mashed potatoes, extra gravy, macaroni and cheese, bread and butter. My mother gives me the elbow. I tell Louise not to feel bad, that I would rather go to the chubby shop if I could have my own room like she does with a four-poster bed and a frilly canopy. Louise says that doesn't make any sense and she's not going shopping anymore. Period.

Louise takes piano lessons. She can play "Malagena"—it's Spanish. Whenever we come over, Aunt Laura makes her play it, and Louise gets nervous and hits a lot of wrong notes. Louise taught me how to read music, and I'm teaching myself to play "Fur Elise." So far, I've got the right hand okay, but the left hand isn't so good. My father says that when we buy the house, we will also buy a piano, and then I can take lessons. My mother looks at me and rolls her eyes.

"What are you making promises to the kid for?"

"Why don't you mind your own business, Tessie? I'm talking to my daughter."

I'm sorry I ever asked for a piano.

I like sleeping under the canopy with Louise. Once I had a dream that I was a princess and my parents were the king and queen of the land. I told Louise about it the next morning, and she said she has that dream every night. I don't believe her. I think she just said that because it was a special dream, and she wanted it for herself. Besides, I don't think people have the same dream, any dream, every single night. Louise lies when it's convenient.

Louise is like Uncle Harry; she likes to be the boss of everything. She says it's her house so she should be in charge. I don't think that's fair, because she never stays over at my house, so I never get my turn to be in charge. She says that if I won't play what she wants, she's going to tell her father that I'm not being nice to her, and that will be the end of staying over. I don't think Uncle Harry would do that, but I'm not going to take any chances, so I pretty much say okay to whatever it is she wants to do.

"Let's play writing books," she says. She picks the subject, and we each go to separate corners of her room and write what we want to be when we grow up. She wrote that she wants to be a teacher, and I said I wanted to be a head doctor.

"What's that?" she asks. "Is that cannibals or something?"

"No. It's what my father says my mother needs."

"Why?"

"So she would be happy and leave him alone," I say.

She looks at me funny.

I want to change the subject, so I tell her I think she would be a good teacher given how she likes to tell kids what to do.

As we get closer and closer to moving, my mother is getting more and more *far-tshadikt*, confused. She stands in the living room holding one *tchotchke* after another, not knowing what to do with them. I try to stay out of her way, so I'm sitting in the kitchen looking at comic books and eating Mallomars. She yells to me to come out of the kitchen, because she wants to tell me something.

"Never," she says, pointing her finger at me for emphasis, "never leave your mother. Promise me that you'll never move away from me. You know," she says under her breath, "your grandmother could die anytime and where will I be? I'll be in *achinvey*, New Jersey."

I am looking forward to going to all-day school. I wonder if that counts as leaving, but I am afraid of the answer so I don't ask. "I promise," I say, afraid not to mean it.

Then I think about Uncle Izzy.

"Uncle Izzy moved to Beacon, and Grandma didn't die," I say. From what I could tell, Uncle Izzy wasn't worried about Grandma. He is happy in Beacon, riding his don't-you-dare-tell-Grandma motorcycle. As if Grandma doesn't know. I don't know why they always think they can hide things from Grandma. If I fall on my face, which I do a lot, I'm *not* to tell Grandma.

"But won't she see the scab?" I ask.

"So what? Just tell her someone at nursery school hit you," my mother says.

I don't understand why getting punched in the face is okay, but falling on your face isn't.

"Why can't I tell Grandma? She knows I have two left feet. Remember when I tripped on the stoop and got a black eye, and Grandma took me to the butcher and bought a steak and put it on my eye? She knows I'm a klutz. I thought you said I was never to keep secrets, so why can't I tell Grandma?"

"Because *Y* is a crooked letter," she says. I have no answer to that, so I shut up, which is the point.

I am upset, thinking that something could happen to Grandma after we move. I tell myself this is just my mother being crazy, because my grandma is very strong. She can lift a big turkey out of the oven all by herself. She can pound a mound of dough until it is soft enough for me to shape into cookies. She can also kill a chicken with one swing by the neck—which is a big yuck as far as I'm concerned, but Grandma says that was when she lived in the *shtetl*, and in Brooklyn you don't have to kill your own chickens. I think my grandma is very pretty. She has the softest skin in the world, because she rubs mineral oil all over. Her hair is brown and white. She wears a girdle with bones under her dress, so she will always be straight as an arrow.

My mother says that Grandma works like a dog. Everybody, all my aunts and uncles and cousins, except for Uncle Izzy, squeezes around the kitchen table, and Grandma serves the chicken soup and the pot roast. My mother and Uncle Seymour yell at her to sit down and eat, but no one lifts a finger to help, so I don't know how they think the food is going to get served if she sits down to eat. Grandma says she is always happy when the family comes over and eats her food, and she looks happy on Saturday. I decide that there is nothing wrong with Grandma, and that my mother is just having a conniption.

I am worried that once we move to Redfield, I won't do any more sleepovers at Grandma's. I stayed over at Grandma's a lot. Whenever my mother "couldn't take it anymore because she had had it up to here," she would drop me off at Grandma's. Sometimes she wouldn't come get me for a week, which was fine with me.

Grandma and I slept in the same bed. Grandpa slept in a different bed, so he didn't mind. I always had the best dreams when I slept at Grandma's, because we'd have heart-to-hearts before I closed my eyes. I would tell her everything that was bothering me, like that I wasn't picked to be Queen Esther in the Chanukah play at school, or that my friend Becca got a Tiny Tears doll but my mother said I can't get one until I'm good.

I asked Grandma how to be good and she says that I am the *goodest* little girl she knows, and we laugh because *goodest* isn't even a word. At Grandma's, I go to sleep happy.

My mother says that when we move to Redfield, I will have my own room with a bed and a dresser and that there will even be room for a big dollhouse.

"How about a Raggedy Andy doll instead of a doll-house?" I ask.

Actually, I want both, but I don't want to be a *chazzer*, a little pig like her sister Ethel who grabbed everything.

"Ask your father," she says. "It's time he bought you something."

Which is the same thing as telling me to go buy it myself. In other words, forget it.

If you want to know the truth, I am more excited about getting out of the crib and having a real bed than I am about getting the dollhouse or a Raggedy Andy.

My mother also says that after we move, we will still go to Grandma's at least once on the weekend and that I will still get to see all my cousins.

"Right, Gerry?" she yells to my father, as a reminder that he has promised to take us every week.

And he does take us without too much complaining. I think he is happier going to Grandma's, because sitting at home with us on the weekend gives him *shpilkes*, restlessness. While everybody is in the kitchen talking over each other, my father sits in the green, flowered wing chair in Grandma's living room. My mother goes in and yells at him to put the paper down and be sociable! He gives her a look and goes back to the paper. The whole ride back to New Jersey she yells how it was all right when her brothers lent him money, but now that he doesn't need them anymore, he doesn't give them the time of day.

"Where's your gratitude?" she asks my father.

At first my father looks like a puppy that pooped on the rug, but then he gets snarly. One time he swerves the car and almost gets us into a big accident. My mother says it's his fault, that he nearly got us killed. My father says it's my mother's fault for driving him crazy. Sometimes I put in my two cents and say whose fault I think it is—usually agreeing with my father—just to distract them so my father won't drive off the road again. My mother says "little *pishers* have big ears" and I should just mind my own beeswax.

"Lay down on the back seat and take a nap," she orders.

Redfield turns out to be pretty nice. We are on the second floor. The apartment has a front door and a back door. We never go in through the front door, because we might track dirt on the rug. Instead, we climb the outside stairs to the landing and go in the back door, onto the kitchen linoleum. The kitchen is big enough for a Formica table and two chairs. The table is where I eat my breakfast—quietly so I don't wake my mother. I make myself Mallomars and milk, and, sometimes, if I have time before I have to leave for school, I make Raisin Bran. Mostly I just have Mallomars. There is a phone on the wall just over the kitchen table where my mother likes to sit, smoke cigarettes, and talk to Grandma or to her new best friend, Rachel.

Rachel has a little girl who becomes my best friend, Roberta, but everybody calls her Bobby. I think Bobby is a weirdo name for a girl, but she likes it, so I call her Bobby, too.

My mother is very excited that I am friends with Bobby, because this means that she and Rachel can send us outside to play at the same time and then they will have *privacy*, which is something my mother can't get enough of, mainly because I watch and listen to everything so I will know when to take cover—like when my mother is on the phone with Rachel, and she starts twirling her wedding band faster and faster and talking lower and lower, I know it's a good time to hightail it outside.

I hear my mother on the phone telling Rachel that my father is always working late. "What the hell was the point of moving to New Jersey to be near his factory if he never comes home anyway? And," she adds "I have serious doubts as to whether he is working at all or just *fooling around*."

I know about the working late, because I hear my mother crying in her bed, but it takes me awhile to understand that *fooling around* doesn't mean acting silly—until I hear her tell Rachel something about Lillian the secretary. Then I remember that day my father, finally—because I kept nagging him—took me to the factory to pick out one of the Junior Miss handbags. Lillian was there and I saw him give her a kiss that didn't look like a friendly hello. He said that they were just *fooling around* and that I shouldn't tell my mother. My mother said that I was supposed to tell her everything, so now I was going to have to keep a secret about keeping a secret. I was very upset, but that had to be a secret, too.

I skip kindergarten and go right to first grade. My mother convinces the principal in Metuchen that I am a very smart kid, and, besides, I've already gone to nursery school, which is just like kindergarten, and there's no point in me repeating it. Also, first grade is all day, and she needs her afternoons to herself. I'm excited to go to first grade, anyway. I *am* smart. I already started to read and write on my own, but I need some help, so it will be good to go the whole day.

"I thought Cousin Louise was the smart one?" I ask when we leave the principal's office.

"What difference does it make who's smarter?"

"I don't know, but I heard you and Aunt Laura saying that I'm the pretty one and Louise is the smart one."

"You know, you are a little *pischer*. You're pretty and you're smart. Now don't go letting that go to your head."

"Does that mean that Louise isn't smart?"

"You know, Linda, you're driving me crazy. Enough already, with the smart and the pretty. You're going to first grade. That's all that matters."

I get Mrs. Frankenheimer for first grade. I like her a lot. Maybe even better than Miss Katz, my nursery school teacher. Mrs. Frankenheimer decides that I don't have such big ears. She notices that she has to keep repeating herself to me. At first, she thinks I'm just not listening, but then she has another idea. She gets my parents to sign a paper allowing me to get a hearing test at school. They figure out that I have a super good right ear but a super bad left ear.

My mother has trouble figuring it out.

She says, "You hear everything you want to hear." She gets on the phone with Rachel.

"I don't know about that test. The kid hears everything she wants to hear, but they want me to take her to the doctor, so I'll take her."

After the doctor, Mrs. Frankenheimer moves me to the front of the class, so I can hear her instructions. I can also read her lips, which I have learned how to do without even knowing I was doing it. The front row also gets me away from William, who spends the whole day making pig noises at me.

The doctor also tells my mother that I must have had a bad ear infection that burst the drum, and now I have scar tissue, and that's why I can't hear out of that ear. He says that I should have had penicillin, because then my drum wouldn't have burst.

I remember the earache. It hurt all night. I was at Grandma's house, but I don't tell my mother this, because I don't want Grandma to get in trouble.

Bobby lives two cul-de-sacs over. We meet up in the middle and then go exploring. We discover a big white house up in the woods behind the village. Bobby's mother tells us that this had been the manor house that once owned all the land, and that the manor people sold the land to the Redfield Village guys who built our apartments. She says she thinks the old lady of the manor still lives in the house.

Bobby and I want to see her. We're curious. We creep up to the house, peek in the windows, and try to get a look at the lady. We decide she might be a wicked witch and if she catches us, she might throw us in the oven like Hansel and Gretel. The house is white clapboard that hasn't been painted in a hundred years. The shutters hang off the hinges. It has a big, black, wrought iron fence and a gate that squeaks whenever we sneak in. The branches from the big walnut trees brush the roof and make moaning sounds in the wind. The house has floor-to-ceiling windows. The drapes are always open a crack and you can see in if you get right up close and put your nose to the glass. We take turns peering through, and, one time, Bobby is sure she sees someone moving around inside. We are determined to see the lady! I start having nightmares about the white house and I don't want to go peeking in those windows anymore, but I don't want Bobby to call me a sissy, so I don't tell about my dreams, and I keep on going.

Bobby and I have different games for different seasons. The fall is skating season. We strap on roller skates and tighten the grips with a key that hangs on a ribbon around our necks. The cul-de-sacs are perfect for skating, because there are only a few cars. When the walnut trees drop their fruit, we scrape out the soft centers, make a hole on the side, stick a straw in and call it a pipe, or we string them together into giant necklaces. In the winter, we play Monopoly at Bobby's house, but it's my set, and I am very particular about keeping all the money lined up and making sure when we're done that the red hotels and green houses and the cards go back in the box, in the exact right place that was meant for them. Bobby says I'm a little nuts having to keep everything just right, but I don't care. I like to be sure that I haven't lost any pieces, and that is that.

My mother is happy that I have Bobby, but she wants me to have more than just one friend. I tell her I have friends at school, but I like Bobby best. I don't want more friends; what I want is a little sister or brother. I ask her if she could please have another baby, but she says what she always says: one of me is enough.

Later, in one of our heart-to-hearts, Grandma tells me that my mother had an operation, and that's why she can't have more children, and she feels very bad about it, so I shouldn't keep asking for a sister or brother. Grandma tells me all about the hospital my mother was in, with a cross of Christ over the bed and all these nuns running around taking care of her.

"When I went to visit your mother," she says, "I just didn't look up." And then she says, "Who knows, maybe Jesus on the cross even helped, because your mother got better and she came home." Grandma tucks the blankets tight under the mattress, making me feel snug and safe in her bed. "Anyway, who's to say? Whatever helped, helped. Besides," Grandma adds, "maybe it wasn't a *shandeh* that Christ hung over your mother's bed, because Christ used to be a Jew, so maybe this time it was okay for your mother to be with the *goyim*."

One day, after I have my Mallomars, I go into the bedroom to wake my mother so she can make my braids; this is our routine. She tells me to remind my father that he has a daughter.

"He knows that," I say.

"Just do as I tell you."

"Okay," I say.

"Give me a kiss," she says.

I don't like the morning kisses. Mommy smells like cigarettes and smoke, but I give her a quick kiss and run out the door.

When I come home from school, Grandma is in our kitchen. This is very surprising, because Grandma never comes to Metuchen; we always go to Brooklyn. Something isn't right. She's wearing my mother's apron. She doesn't smile, but she does give me a big hug.

"Where's Mommy?" I ask. Grandma purses her lips and looks somewhere else.

"She's in the hospital, but she is going to be okay."

"What happened?"

"I don't know," she says, meaning she's not going to tell me.

"Is she in the hospital with the *goyim*?" I ask.

"No, not this time."

Grandma pulls something out of the oven and even through the pot holder glove, it burns her. She almost drops the pan onto the stovetop.

"You okay?" I ask. "Where's Daddy?"

"Where's your father? You tell me—where's your father?" Grandma bangs the pan onto the stove. "I don't know where anything is in this kitchen!" she says, and then turns away from me. I hear her sniffling.

"Are you crying, Grandma?"

"No, sweetheart. I just have a cold." I can tell she is lying.

My mother comes home the next day, but she doesn't answer my questions either. Grandma says to just let her be, so I call Bobby and ask her if she wants to go skating in the cul-de-sac. I want Grandma to sleep over so that we can have a heart-to-heart before bed, because I know if we do she will tell me at least enough to make me feel better. But she has to get home to Brooklyn.

It's like magic. My father starts coming home at night. My mother makes steak and peas. We set the table and eat in the dining room. I look at my mother. My mother looks at my father. My father doesn't bring the newspaper to the table. My mother asks him about his day. "Okay," he says. She asks about orders for pocketbooks. "Okay," is all he answers.

That night after Mom cooks dinner is the first night I have the dream. I am an astronaut walking in space. I am connected to the big spaceship by a long, thick rope. In the spaceship, I float up by the ceiling. I open the door and float out into the dark. I want to see the stars. Suddenly I feel a tug, hear a ripping sound, and the rope has broken. *"Momma!"* I yell for help. *"Grandma!"* I yell, but nobody hears me. I tumble and fall and somersault; I'm dizzy; I float. I see the spaceship move farther and farther away. I should never have left the spaceship. Everything is very, very quiet. Everything is very, very black. No one can hear me. No one can see me. I know now I'm going to float out here forever, alone in the dark.

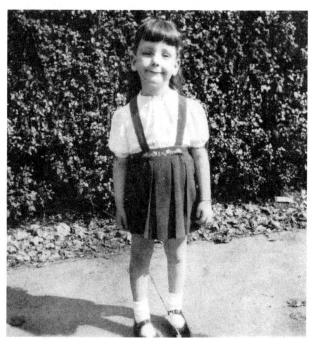

Linda at age 4

⌒ outside the frame ⌒

There is a black and white photo of my mother and me, taken in front of our apartment building on Avenue H in Brooklyn—a six-story building with white, Greek columns as incongruous as my parents' marriage. The apartment had two distinguishing features—a step-down living room or step-up dining room, depending upon your perspective, and a railroad El running outside our kitchen window. If the train was going slow, we could see the faces of the people sitting in the cars; if it was going fast, all the dishes in the cupboard rattled. I liked to sit in my highchair and wait for the *choo-choo*. I liked the whistle. I thought the train was a large toy, but my mother thought it was a noisy pain in the ass. My mother looks pretty in the picture—decked out in a figure-hugging suit with a peplum jacket and platform heels. You can tell by her stride that she is determined to get where she is going. Her eyes face forward. She is gripping the handle of my pram, a beautiful, sleek, black carriage with a large hood and spoke wheels, typical of fine baby carriages in the forties.

I am toddling after her, trying to catch up. A large sunflower bonnet hides my face. My legs are bowed, my feet pigeon-toed, which was how my mother always described my little girl body. I never quite believed that this particular configuration was possible. What the picture suggests is that this deformity was not necessarily congenital, but more likely attributable to the diaper hanging low between my knees. If you look closely at the photograph, you can see the head of a collie pup poking out from under the hood of the pram. The dog's name is Penny.

Penny, preferring to pee and poop in the comfort of her new home, refused, despite my mother's cajoling, to step one paw outside the apartment door. Taking me out of the carriage putting the dog in was Tessie's ingenious solution to getting her out of the house—the next best idea was to get rid of the dog altogether, an outcome that would inevitably come to pass.

Penny was a rescue dog in the metaphorical sense of the word. My mother said she needed a dog like a *loch en kup*, a hole in the head, but she was desperate to please Gerry, and hoped that his desire for a dog would translate to a desire for her. She was willing to put up with the poop and the pee if her husband would just come home in the evenings. She imagined him sitting in his easy chair, reading the paper, smoking his pipe, and petting the dog.

This picture of what she imagined is *not* to be found in the family album. My father, after a long day wheeling and dealing in the garment center, preferred to spend his evenings where he knew he would be admired and appreciated—at Longchamps Bar in the lobby of the Empire State Building, where he fielded come-ons from women unable to resist his wink and smile. The only woman my father had trouble managing was Tessie. Hurt and angry that he didn't come home, she berated him when he did, which drove my father back to the bar. It was a vicious cycle that no dog—or for that matter, no *kid*—was going to change.

I had an affinity for Penny. She and I were in the same sinking ship. Penny had failed in her mission as I had failed in mine. My mother often told me that I had been conceived to keep my father out of the army. When it turned out he was 4F, I wasn't needed after all. My mother reinvented my purpose— if she herself wasn't going to be the draw for my father, then maybe I would. To fulfill this role, it was imperative that I be both charming and beautiful. Making a scrawny, pigeon-toed, bow-legged little kid into a seductive beauty was not easy. The hope was that I'd improve with age, but she had serious doubts, and her anxiety was contagious.

My mother tried desperately to fatten me up, but I resisted. She cooked lamp chops and mashed potatoes for dinner and banana sandwiches for lunch, but I would play with my food and toss the bone to Penny. I wouldn't poop either. Feeling at the mercy of her machinations, I exercised control wherever I could. Days would go by, and I'd refuse to cooperate.

"I'm throwing up my hands. I'm fed up to here," she would say, slicing a finger across her neck for emphasis. "What am I going to do with you?"

She phoned her mother for help. My grandmother, a very practical lady, told my mother to calm down and give me some mineral oil. I don't think it was the mineral oil that made the difference, but simply that I would do anything for my grandma. I loved her like no one else.

The one-bedroom apartment on Avenue H had been an excellent first apartment for the bride and groom, but not so good when the kid came along. My crib was placed at the foot of their bed. Freud would have legitimately argued that the seeds of my neurosis could be traced back to the placement of my crib. It was there that I languished for five years—the plastic baby mattress with the little doll print is indelibly etched in my psyche.

In the mornings, assuming he had come home the night before, my father would rush out the door. I would lie awake, sucking my thumb—legs dangling between the bars like skinny branches off a new tree, waiting for my mother to get up and release me from my pen. Don't ask me why I didn't just climb out and go about my business, whatever that may have been. It would have been easy enough, but something told me that my cooperation in the misadventure of my existence was imperative. It took a death-defying stomach virus and my pediatrician, Dr. Maslow, to finally spring me from my cage.

In the Jewish homeopathy of the day, the prescription for diarrhea and vomiting was lox. The logic was that salty lox would induce thirst, causing you to drink and not dehydrate. Unless, that is, you're fed Nova—the non-salty lox. I don't know which lox I was forced to eat, but at three in the morning, an emergency phone call was made to Dr. Maslow. He came with two bottles of intravenous fluid, stuck a needle in each dangling leg, and instructed my mother on one side and my father on the other, to hold up the bottles. Then he proceeded to berate them for keeping me caged like an animal. I was too distraught with my medical predicament to appreciate his calling them to task, but less than a year later, it was announced that we were moving to Metuchen, New Jersey.

I did not get the promised bed; I got a Castro Convertible. My mother hoped that a member of her family, preferably her mother, would *shlep* out from Brooklyn and visit us in God-forsaken New Jersey. She said it was imperative that my bedroom be a guest room-sitting room. The bed went back to the top of my wish list, followed by my desire for a pet—by this time Penny had been donated to the ASPCA where she, as had I, languished in a pen. I made do with a yo-yo that I pulled behind me like something on a leash. While the kid in the Castro commercial was fourteen and able to open the bed with ease, I was six, and every night when I hauled the cushions off the couch and yanked the bed from its casing, I nearly tore my arms out of their sockets. When I complained, my mother asked if I'd rather be back in the crib. This did not seem like a fair choice. In consolation, she bought me the desired Raggedy Andy doll, which sat floppily on the couch—a constant reminder of my cousin Louise's four-poster. I might add that only once did Grandma come to stay at our house. Throughout the six years we lived in Metuchen, I harbored sincere concerns that I might go the way of the dog. I was not turning into the beauty Tessie hoped for, and my father had as much interest in playing with me as he'd had in petting the dog. My anxiety rose to a pitch, and I kept tripping over my own two feet.

There is another picture in the album, taken in the cul-de-sac of our garden apartment. I stand leaning against my blue, Schwinn two-wheeler. I am about nine years old. My hair is cut too short, and my bangs are crooked, making my right eye look higher than the left. One leg of my jeans is rolled up, revealing a shin covered in scabs. I am holding a football. Maybe I'd decided that my best chance for longevity in this family rested in trying to be the son my father wished he had had rather than the daughter my mother could have done without.

In sixth grade, against my wishes, she registered me for Mrs. Maple's dance class at the YMCA. She made me a black, velvet dress with a white, puritan collar and bought me a pair of little white gloves with tiny pearl buttons at the wrist. After the first lesson, I begged my mother for a reprieve. I resented having to sit, hands folded in my lap, legs crossed at the ankle, waiting patiently for a boy to come across the room and select me, bow cordially, and ask me to dance. I complained to my mother that girls should be able to pick their partners too, and, had I been given that option, I would never have been stuck dancing with William, the class jerk. Tessie said that I didn't know how to act like a lady. I said that was because I was a kid, and I didn't want to be a lady if that's how ladies had to act. My attitude failed to improve, and soon the boys stopped asking me to dance. I became a wallflower, which was just fine with me.

When I was in seventh grade, my father's fortunes went south again, and we left Metuchen and moved to a shabby garden apartment in Floral Park, Queens. I had two friends—sisters Inez and Daphne—whom I looked up to, but couldn't compete with. They were from Latvia and seemed misplaced in Queens. They were blonde bombshells with big breasts and curvy hips. This was the time of the Marilyn Monroe pin-up—Twiggy had yet to arrive on the scene. Though I was fourteen, puberty seemed to have skipped over me, and the contrast between me and the Latvian sisters was almost more than my mother could bear. Her looks of anticipation changed to glares of accusation. Was I spiting her with my body—holding back now as I had when I was in diapers? In a panic, she took me to her gynecologist. Together they examined me. Why my mother was in the room, let alone between my legs, is beyond me, but together they decided that, although slow, my body was not hopeless, and that sometime soon I would be blessed with *the curse*.

Shortly thereafter, I ran to my mother with blood on my hands. I expected a big smile and a tight hug, but, in another inexplicable expression of Jewish ritual, I got a slap in the face. When asked *why* in the world, my mother, not knowing the answer, responded as usual, "*Y* is a crooked letter," handed me some Modess pads, and warned me that I better keep my privates private. Tessie expected that when my period came, my resistance would go, and I would embrace young womanhood. I did wear poodle skirts and scream after Elvis, but my favorite outfit was still blue jeans and my father's white shirt, rolled up at the cuffs. It still seemed to me that boys got the better deal: in gym, boys were given the choice between real sports like football and basketball, while girls chose between square dancing and home economics. I could master the do-si-do or boil eggs. My mother said I'd better learn to boil eggs, because she was getting mighty tired of cooking for a man who doesn't come home. That didn't make any sense but I didn't want to argue.

In my freshman year of high school, the choices improved—girls could now play volleyball or half-court basketball, two dribbles and then shoot. These rules were meant to protect menstruating girls who were assumed to be in a weakened condition—another reason periods were a curse. I was considered tall at the time—five foot seven and still growing. My mother, sure that boys would be unwilling to look up to me, half-seriously suggested that I walk around the house with books on my head to stunt my growth. I refused and decided instead to use my height to my advantage. I tried out for the girls' basketball team and became the center forward. I have no memory of either of my parents coming to my games.

No sooner had I settled into high school than it was announced that we were moving back to Brooklyn. Devastated to be the new kid on the block once again, I was promised a dog. Candy, the collie with colitis, became a fast friend. She was my pillow in bed every night. Whenever my parents fought, we huddled together for comfort.

As it turned out, the move wasn't so bad. There were five other teenagers on the street, and four were boys. It was there that I met my new best friend, Phyllis, who was fully into the girl thing and pulled me right in with her. My feminist leanings went into dormancy, and all my energy was directed towards looking attractive and getting boys to like me.

There is a snapshot of me, taken by Phyllis, in the backyard of our new apartment. I am fifteen. I am sitting, posed for the camera on a blanket, in a one-piece, hot-pink bathing suit. My hair is in a flip, and my headband matches the suit. My long legs are crossed at the ankle—back straight as a rod. I have big eyes and small features. Phyllis had the boys from the block drape around me like a lei.

It was around this time that Gerry discovered he had a daughter. He began to come home for dinner. At first my mother was happy—her project of shaping me into a seductive young lady capable of attracting my father had finally come to fruition. However, when she decided to join us on our regular evening walks, she was relegated to bringing up the rear. Her excitement for our newfound affection quickly waned. I, on the other hand, was thrilled with the long-sought-after paternal attention, though it was guilty pleasure. We would walk, and my father would talk about his business problems as if I were a smart adult capable of helping with difficult grownup decisions—I had become his confidante and partner. When my father invited me into the city to meet him at Longchamp's, my mother objected.

"I thought you wanted me to spend time with her?" he argued. "So now I do, and you object. There is no pleasing you."

My mother didn't know what to say. I took the train into Manhattan. My father was a magnet. All the women wanted to be near him, but *I* was his date for the evening. He introduced me to Marge, with the long neck and red bouffant hair, and Sheila, who worked in his office, and others whose names I don't remember. He never referred to me as his daughter; I was his young friend Linda. I soon realized that I was there for his enhancement and not my own. I never wanted to believe my mother, but the evidence in the bar was becoming too close to a truth I still wanted to deny. I became increasingly uncomfortable and began to feel sorry for my mother. It was sad to see that she had lost for winning.

I told my father I wanted to go home.

"Why?" he said.

"Because Mom is waiting."

Sheila was sitting on the stool, on my coat. I asked her to please get up. I grabbed my coat and started putting it on. My father leaned over and gave her a kiss on the cheek, shrugging his shoulders.

We walked out of the bar, my father trailing behind me.

"What's your rush?" he said.

"I told you. Mom is waiting."

⌒ to the mountain ⌒

Between my junior and senior years of high school in Brooklyn, I spent the summer of '57 up at Sader's Bungalow Colony, helping my grandmother run the concession. Bungalow colonies were summer *shtetls*. Jews, happy to escape the Cossacks, but missing home, recreated their home villages in the Borscht Belt in the Catskill Mountains. Sometimes whole cemetery clubs—*lantsmen* from the old country—would come to stay at the same bungalow colony. It wasn't enough that they were going to be together for eternity, they should still be together for the summer. The bungalows—little, one-story cabins—dotted the landscape around the main house the way houses in the *shtetl* clustered around the synagogue. People who couldn't afford a bungalow but still wanted to get out of the city for the summer stayed in the main house. For half the price of a bungalow, they got one room, a bathroom down the hall, and a shared kitchen. Sharing a kitchen led to fights like, "Who took my blueberries?" or "That was my fish!" Thank God that a free bungalow for Grandma and me came with the concession.

The concession sold cigarettes, newspapers, and sundries. There was a soda fountain where Grandma made malteds and egg creams, but that was it. There were no real stores at Sader's. Every time you put your *toches* down in a chair, another peddler came, and you had to go get the cheese from the dairyman or the meat from the traveling butcher. When the blouse man came, you ran like a chicken; you shouldn't miss a bargain. You stood around the peddler's cart trying on this one and that one, always with an eye to see what Selma liked. If Selma said it was good, then it was. Every bungalow colony had a *macher*, a big shot. Selma was the *macher* at Sader's.

But Selma didn't buy from the peddler. Why should she? There wasn't a weekend that her Herbie didn't bring her a present from the city. Like everybody said, Selma and Herbie were "sitting pretty." They had an apartment on Ocean Parkway in Brooklyn, an apartment in Florida on the water, and, in summer, the big bungalow at Sader's with the wrap-around porch and the best view. There was nothing humble about Selma and Herbie.

Aside from me, there were no teenagers at Sader's. Had it not been for my best friend, Phyllis, who stayed with her mother at a bungalow colony the next town over, I would surely have died of boredom. Phyllis had a pretty face, great skin, and no eyebrows. She said they didn't have enough of an arch, so she shaved them off and drew on new ones with dark brown Maybelline pencil. They looked like marionette eyebrows, but I didn't want to hurt her feelings, so I kept my mouth shut. Because Phyllis was a little on the chubby side, her mother fed her diet pills. Phyllis would call me up and want to talk for hours. Sometimes I'd have to just say bye and hang up the phone. She was so wound up on those pills that even after I'd hung up, she probably kept on jabbering. I didn't see why her weight was an issue, because Shelly, her boyfriend, was fatter than she was, and he thought Phyllis looked just fine.

Shelly came up to visit Phyllis in the mountains because they were having sex, and she said he didn't want to miss any. Phyllis was my second friend to lose her virginity. My friend

Sharon lost it first. Sharon was a kewpie doll—short with a small waist and big breasts. She had dimples and blond hair and three dates a night. The boys lined up to date Sharon. My mother said Sharon had gone in the wrong direction. Phyllis and I didn't care what direction she'd gone in; all we knew was she was getting all the dates. When Sharon got pregnant, I didn't tell my mother because she would have declared it a victory, as in "your mother is always right." Sharon moved away after she got pregnant, and that was that for Sharon.

Shelly had a cousin named Ralph Lifshitz. Ralph was staying at his parents' summerhouse in Monticello, which was only twenty-five minutes from Sader's. Ralph was nineteen and had a driver's license. Shelly said that he'd fix me up with Ralph, and we'd all go on a double date.

"It's not going to work," I said to Phyllis.

"What do you mean? You haven't even met him."

"You said he lives in the Bronx."

"Yeah, so?" she said.

"Well, I live in the wrong direction," I said, "because the Bronx doesn't go to Brooklyn."

Phyllis was silent for a minute, and then, in an effort to be encouraging, said, "If you hit it off, and you *will* hit it off, he'll schlep. Trust me on that—if a guy is getting what he wants, he'll schlep. Look at Shelly. Every weekend, he's taking the Trailways to Monticello."

What Phyllis said made me nervous, but I didn't tell her, because she was ahead of me, and she thought I needed to hurry up already.

They came to pick me up at eight. They were supposed to be there by seven, but Shelly said that Phyllis kept erasing her eyebrows. I'd been ready since five, and I would have been ready even earlier except that I kept fixing my hair. I had one of those bouffant hairdos. The bouffant was about as practical as a girdle. You had to start working on it the night before by sleeping, or trying to sleep, with your hair wrapped in toilet paper around these big fat rollers. When you combed it out, you had to pull it straight, then tease it up and turn it under. When you were done, it looked like you had a hair helmet. I also kept changing my outfit from pedal pushers to poodle skirt, back to pedal pushers. Every time I changed, I had to fix my hair. It was making me crazy.

When they finally pulled up, I took a deep breath and then took my time walking over to the car; they shouldn't think I was on pins and needles. Ralph, my date for the night, was coming around the back of the Chevy to open up the door on my side. He was stunning, nothing like the boys at my high school with their duck's ass hairdos or James Dean motorcycle boots. Ralph Lifshitz was no greaser. He had class. He wore a crisp, white, linen shirt that someone had just ironed, with the cuffs turned up. He had on khaki Bermuda shorts, and no socks with his penny loafers. As he reached out to open my door, I saw his silver I.D. bracelet with his engraved initials. I'd only known him for five seconds and I was already envisioning walking into class in September wearing that bracelet.

"Linda," he said, looking straight in my eyes, "pleasure to meet you." And then he gave me a peck on the cheek. He was smooth and his smile was sexy, and I didn't know if he was being polite or being forward, but I didn't care. He was the only college I wanted to go to.

"You're so tan," I said, and then thought it a dumb thing to say. Of course he was; it was summer.

"Tennis," he said. Nobody I knew played tennis. Stoop ball, stickball, dodge ball, but not tennis.

As he drove, he covered the basics, confirming what Phyllis had already told me, that he lived on Mosholu Parkway in the Bronx, had two older brothers and a sister. His father was an artist, and his mother stayed home and cooked and cleaned house.

"What kind of artist?" I asked.

"He goes to rich people's apartments and paints murals in their dining rooms and hallways."

"What kind of murals?" I'd never seen painted murals in apartments in Brooklyn. Maybe it was a Bronx thing.

"Pictures of the English countryside," Ralph said. I smiled and nodded as if I knew what that looked like.

Ralph said his parents had been coming up to the country since he was a baby, and he knew all the back roads and hidden trails. "Who knows?" he said, "maybe someday I'll take you for a hike to the top of the mountain, and show you one of my favorite spots in all of the Catskills. There's a big rock at the top, and when you climb up on that rock and look down, you can see the Concord Hotel—the richest hotel in the Catskills—or look up, and see the Big Dipper and Orion's Belt."

I tried to do what Phyllis would do: I gave him a *come on* smile and asked, "Is that a tease or a promise?"

He smiled back at me, and I could tell he liked my sass.

"Where to?" Ralph asked, through the rearview mirror, directed at Shelly in the back seat, but Shelly and Phyllis were busy making out. We drove up and around the mountains with no particular destination in mind. It was fine with me. My eyes were fixated on Ralph's thigh muscle as it tensed each time he hit the brake, and on the beauty of his hands as they turned the steering wheel. There was nothing about him that I didn't like.

He parked the car on Main Street in Monticello. Ralph and I got out, giving Phyllis and Shelly time to put themselves back together. Then we all walked to a chrome diner with a soda fountain, and I slipped into one side of a wide booth with red leather seats. Ralph slipped in beside me, really close. Still too excited to eat, I ordered a vanilla malted. He ordered a Reuben sandwich and a Coke. Phyllis and Shelley had a feast: burgers, fries, and big pieces of pie for dessert. Phyllis asked Shelly for a quarter—I guess sex gives you the right to ask the boy for whatever—and she fed it to the miniature jukebox that sat on our table. Looking at me and then at Ralph, she chose Doris Day singing "If I Give My Heart to You." I'd already given it, and Phyllis knew it.

"I'll call you," is what he said when he dropped me off. He'd written my number down on a piece of paper he found in the glove box. He'd tucked it in his shorts pocket. I couldn't tell if he was politely brushing me off or if he really meant it.

Phyllis spoke to Shelly later, and Shelly said Ralph meant it.

After that night, I divided my time between the porch at the main house and the soda counter inside the concession. The main house had a radio; the concession had the telephone. I'd lie on the porch swing and incessantly turn the radio dial, listening for Elvis singing "Love Me Tender." When I found it, I sang along in this false baritone.

I wanted Ralph Lifshitz to love me tender and true. I wanted him to never let me go.

With my singing, the yentas couldn't concentrate on their mahjong; two cracks, three bam, two flowers. There was usually harmony in the click of the tiles, but I couldn't relax. Finally, the yentas had had it. I was ruining their concentration. They yelled to my grandmother that her granddaughter had lost her mind, and that she should send me back to the city to my mother. That was it for the main house. There was no way I was going back to the city as long as Ralph was in the country. I gave up on the radio, went back to the concession, and sat on the stool, staring at the telephone, willing it to ring.

It was the *only* telephone at Sader's, and it got plenty of use. When you wanted something from the city, you had to come to the concession to use the phone. When a call came in, Grandma would announce it over the loudspeaker, and everybody would know that you had a phone call. It was good to get phone calls. It meant that you were important, that you had business to do and things to take care of. No surprise that Selma got most of the calls. I think she told Herbie to tell people to call her just so she'd look good. I sat there listening to her yack away. She was tying up the phone, and, even if Ralph *were* trying to call me, he wouldn't get through. I kept asking Grandma for change to play the pinball machine, so the *ka-ching* sound of the pinballs would drive her up the wall and off the phone. I sent her all the bad vibrations I could muster until she finally glared at me and gave up.

All the time I waited for his call, I pictured us in a tight embrace, his hand pulling my head towards his kiss, his tongue exploring the inside of my mouth. He would know how to do it. We would be Burt Lancaster and Deborah Kerr—their beach would be our mountain. Warm feelings churned deep inside my belly. I hadn't known these feelings before.

"That's passion," Phyllis said. "That's what you feel when you are really turned on."

"I'm an idiot," I said. "I should have known all this. I'm sixteen. I feel like I've been living under a rock."

"Well it's time to come out. That's what I've been telling you. Ralph's perfect. He's just the guy to do it," she said.

Each day he didn't call me, I became more despondent. I kept calling Phyllis and begging her to ask Shelly what he knew about Ralph. Phyllis said that Shelly wasn't the one to ask.

"So then, who?" I asked.

"I don't know. You just have to wait."

"Easy for you to say," I told her. "You have Shelly."

"No, I don't. We broke up."

"What?" I screamed into the phone. "You can't break up! How am I going to know what I need to know? You can't break up. That's simply unacceptable. What happened?" I wailed.

"I didn't want to do it," she said.

"Do what?"

"That mouth thing," she said.

"What?"

"You know," she said, "where you put his thing into your mouth until, you know . . . it's over."

I was exasperated. "What's your problem?" I said. "You have no problem stuffing things into your mouth! That's why you have to take those diet pills. So go take a pill and call Shelly."

Phyllis hung up on me. I guess it was mean what I said, but I didn't see why she would do everything else, but not this. If they stayed broken up, I might never have any info on Ralph Lifshitz again. I finally gave up, put on my bathing suit, grabbed a towel, and went down to the pond for a swim.

At Sader's everybody else hung around the pool. I hated the pool. It was a small rectangular cement hole. The bottom was painted blue so the water would look like the Mediterranean. But it just looked fake, and you could smell the chlorine from a hundred yards away. Dyed blonde hair turned green by the end of the summer, and the women started wearing babushkas to cover their heads, so no one would find out they were bottle blondes. The pond had a silky bottom that made your toes curl. There were turtles and frogs and low-hung trees. It always smelled fresh, *alive*, as if it had just rained, and best of all, no one was ever there. I floated on my back and picked out faces in the clouds. For a half hour, I didn't think of Ralph. Or I did, but it was pleasant, not painful, and I wasn't staring at a phone but at a beautiful summer sky, the same sky that held the stars he wanted to show me from his mountaintop. When I got back to the concession, I felt more like myself. I was shaking the water out of my left ear when Grandma said, "Your fellow called."

I couldn't believe it. How was it possible? I was gone for only a half hour.

"Ralph Lifshitz?" I said.

She nodded. "Who else?" she said. "You have some other boy, too?"

"*What did he say?*"

"He said 'Hello.' He asked for Linda. I said you were out. He said okay and he'd call back later. He said thank you—a very polite boy."

"Later? When? Did he say when *later*?"

"No," Grandma said. "Why should he have to say when? When he'll call, he'll call."

Since Grandpa died, Grandma had rejoiced in the pleasures of celibacy and tried to get some of it to rub off on me. I couldn't help it—all my adolescent energy was pushing me away from celibacy and straight toward debauchery. I slumped down to the puddle I had dripped on the floor. The phone rang. I popped up to answer it. It was for Selma. I hated Selma.

That was Friday. Don't even ask me about that weekend. I just moped around the grounds ready to bolt to the concession if Grandma announced the phone was for me. Phyllis wasn't talking to me except to tell me that I'd thrown her to the dogs. She said that I wouldn't do *it* either and that I should stop acting like a big shot because I hadn't done *anything*, so what was I even talking about? Phyllis was right. I didn't know anything. I was going to be a senior in high school and I'd only been to second base. Ezra Cohen had touched my breast, but I had my sweater on, so I don't know if that even counted.

When I was walking by the pool I saw that Selma had strategically left a copy of *Peyton Place* wide open on her beach chair, so everybody would see that she was a sexpot. I grabbed the book and went and hid it in my room. I'd heard about this book and figured that maybe I could find out what Phyllis was making such a fuss about. By the time I finished the book, I knew more, but I didn't really understand how the whole *it* thing worked. It didn't matter because Phyllis and Shelly were back together, and the lines of communication were reopened. I'm not sure what compromises had been made, but harmony was restored.

Ralph finally called on Wednesday. We went out for three nights in a row, twice with Phyllis and Shelly and then, finally, just us. Ralph was very sure about everything. It wasn't attitude. It was just certainty. I didn't have to work hard to believe him. I just knew if he said it, it was true. He taught me a lot of important stuff. He said Elvis was teenage crap and that if I wanted to listen to real music, I should listen to this, and he held up Sinatra's comeback album, *Come Fly with Me*. Any song on that album, he said, was better than any of that rock and roll garbage. He told me to get rid of the teased-out hairdo and just let my hair hang long and straight. He said he wasn't going back to CCNY in the fall, that he had big plans and no time for college. I shouldn't ask what his plans were— he'd tell me when he'd tell me. Then he asked if I was ready to climb the mountain with him. I thought he was proposing so I immediately said, "yes." In a second, I realized that he meant the trail to the rock, not the key to his heart.

"Next Saturday night, eight o'clock," he said. "Wear sneakers."

By Saturday night I was so excited, I couldn't sit still. I made sure to dress simply—blue jeans with a denim shirt tied at the waist, and sneakers—and to let my hair hang straight and loose. Ralph smiled when he saw me, so I guess I fit the bill. I raised a finger to tell him to wait a minute. I ran into the concession to give Grandma a kiss good bye. She couldn't come out from behind the counter because she was busy making an egg cream for Selma's husband, Herbie.

"Have a good time, *mameleh*," she said, "and don't be too late."

"Maybe it's too late already," Herbie said with a sleaze-ball laugh.

I gave him a dirty look and ran out to the car.

I waved goodbye to Selma and the other yentas who were craning their necks to see into the car. He was driving his older brother's '56 Chevy. It was red with cream-colored leather seats. I was going to ask how his brother could afford such a nice car, but I didn't want to be nosey. Ralph rolled down the windows with an automatic button on his side of the car. My hair blew in the wind.

Ralph held my hand as we drove, his middle finger occasionally stroking my palm. I lifted his hand and ran my tongue over his knuckles. He tasted like salt and smelled like soap. We drove through Monticello and then up a narrow country road. When it turned to dirt, he pulled the car over and helped me out. We walked along the edge until he found a small opening in the brush. It was the trail that led to the top of the mountain. His favorite place. We began the ascent. The trail was narrow and rocky. At times, the branches of the trees formed a canopy, blocking out what little light came from the sliver of moon. Such darkness. Ralph held my forearm, steering me as if he were pulling a little red wagon. He pointed to the ground whenever a tree root threatened to trip me. I loved him.

When we got to the top, the sky opened like a curtain on a celestial stage. The stars were white flowers appliquéd with silver thread on a black velvet sky. I *was* in heaven.

The night was cool. The air smelled like pine. It was like being in a dream, a really good dream. Ralph directed my gaze to the Big Dipper, as he unbuttoned my blouse and helped me off with my jeans. The bra went. The panties too. I'd never been naked with a boy before. Never been naked outside, either. I climbed off the rock and ran in wide circles with my arms out, feeling the breeze kiss my skin. Ralph laughed. He had taken off his shirt but he still had on his shorts. Was it my imagination or was the moonlight glinting off his beautiful chest? When he got naked, I couldn't help but stare. I tried to act casual, but I wanted to examine every part of him. He was beautiful all over.

"Watch out," he said as I spun around, "There's a nunnery on that other hilltop. Stay out of the moonlight."

Even the mention of nuns, church, religion, didn't faze me.

When I came back to the rock, he slipped his shirt around my shoulders to keep me warm and began to kiss me deep and caress my thighs.

"I need to ask you something," he said. "Are you a virgin?"

I thought about what he was asking and I was confused.

"Do you mean have I ever done *any*thing or have I never done *every*thing?"

My hesitation and confusion was all the answer he needed. He stopped touching me.

"What's wrong?" I asked, suddenly shivering.

"I don't sleep with virgins," he said.

"Why?" I asked. I was relieved but mostly disappointed. "I have to lose my virginity with someone, and I'd like it to be you," I said.

"Too much responsibility," he said, and kissed me on the cheek.

"There are other things we can do," I said, thinking of Phyllis.

I pushed him back down on the rock. I slid down to where his hair began to tickle my face. I had decided to do *it*. I wished that I had asked Phyllis for a better description—more direction. I was scared and I didn't really know what I was doing. I fumbled around. I felt Ralph's excitement wane. He gently lifted my head.

"Get dressed. Let's go," he said.

I didn't know if I'd just been rejected or respected. His desire snagged on a technicality. Climbing down the mountain, I felt awful. I felt sick.

When he dropped me off at Sader's, he gave me a peck on the lips and a pat on the back. "That was fun," he said, and smiled, but I didn't believe him for one second.

It was two weeks until the end of the summer. I moped around, not knowing what to do with myself. I didn't even bother going down to the pond. What was the point? I'd even stopped listening for the phone. He wasn't going to call. It was over.

Grandma felt sorry for me. She kept making up jobs for

me to do so I'd keep busy. She even got the yentas to teach me mahjong. That actually distracted me for a while, but they played a fast game, and I was too slow. I decided I was too slow at everything. Phyllis had been telling me that all through junior year. Had I listened to Phyllis, I could have taken my sweater off and had sex with Ezra Cohen, and then I wouldn't have been a virgin, and then maybe Ralph would have been willing to schlep to Brooklyn the way Shelly schlepped to the mountains.

I saw Ralph one more time over the Labor Day weekend. I wanted to see him alone, but Phyllis and Shelly had planned for the four of us to have an end-of-the-summer bash. He seemed happy to see me. He gave me the usual peck on the cheek, but he didn't take my hand when we were driving. We went back to the diner, and this time Phyllis told me to pick the song. I played Sinatra singing "Moonlight in Vermont." I felt a little better when I saw Ralph smile.

Back in Brooklyn, all was silent. Not a word. Month after month, I kept calling him. His mother always answered sweetly and in a Yiddish accent said, "I'm sorry, dahling, but my Ralphie isn't home. What can I tell you? You want I should tell him that you called *again?*"

I gave a sheepish "No, thank you," and went back to bed. I had bought the forty-five single of Little Anthony and the Imperials singing "Tears on My Pillow." I played it over and over. Phyllis said I was pathetic and I should get up and get over it. The whole senior year passed this way. Guys asked me out but they were either greasers or nerds. The guy I wanted was in the Bronx, not in Brooklyn.

I didn't want to go to the senior prom. I wasn't in the mood, but Phyllis said I had to go because she didn't want to go alone. I said, "I thought you were going with Shelly."

"Exactly," she said.

She fixed me up with this guy, Elliot. There was nothing attractive about Elliot. In the pictures my mother took, I'm sitting on the couch with my dress spread out around me. I look like an orange lampshade without the tassels. The dress is taffeta, strapless, with a matching orange orchid wristlet. The smile is fake. Elliot is standing behind me with both hands gripping my shoulders. Too tightly. His tuxedo is blue with black lapels. He smiles wide, showing all the braces on his teeth.

My mother finally stopped with the photo shoot, and we went to the prom. Elliot hovered around, waiting for me to want to dance. Shelly was stationed at the food table. Phyllis and I sat in a huddle, nastily gossiping about everybody's dresses. There was a fanfare. We looked up, and in came Susie, the queen of the prom, on a paper-mache float. The float was silver and gold; her dress was fluffy white chiffon. She looks like Glinda the Good Witch in the Wizard of Oz. She's even waving a wand. We decided we loved the dress.

Just before I graduated, my father had announced that he was having a *situation*, and there was no money for the rent, much less college tuition. My mother and I, my father, and our collie dog with colitis all piled into Grandma's one-bedroom apartment. It was smaller than the bungalow at Sader's. I had to get out of there. If I couldn't go to college, then I'd have to figure another way out.

I got a job working for Century of Boston, a women's sportswear house that specialized in sweater sets and four-gore skirts. Century was located at 1407 Broadway, the heart of the garment district. It was a scene in the lobby. Salesmen and buyers in pinstripe suits, star sapphire pinky rings, and sunglasses stood around reading *Women's Wear Daily* and trying to look like they mattered. The secretaries and showroom girls clicked by in their high-heeled shoes, smiled prettily, and for a moment, made them think that they did. I got hired on as a showroom model and receptionist. I was five foot eight inches tall with long, thin legs. I had taken Ralph's advice and stopped teasing my hair. It hung loose onto my shoulders. I was too naïve to know that it was my looks and not my intelligence that got me the job.

When I was the receptionist, I sat at a desk behind a sliding glass window, fielding come-ons from textile salesmen trying to get in to see the designer. When I was a model, I slinked around the showroom trying to look like Suzy Parker and make the garments hang right for the buyers. The job paid seventy-five dollars a week and had the kind of glamour that impresses an eighteen-year-old girl only two generations away from a tenement on the Lower East Side.

Every morning I stood on the El, waiting for the train to take me out of Brooklyn. I came alive when I climbed the subway steps onto Broadway. If I couldn't be a college coed, then I'd be a New York City career girl. One night when I came home and everyone was in their usual places—Grandma at the kitchen sink, my mother smoking a cigarette and stewing at the kitchen table, and my father nowhere to be seen—I said I had an announcement.

"I have good news. You'll soon have more room here."

"Why? Are you planning to kill the dog?" my mother said, with only half a smile.

"Very funny. I've decided to move to New York City. It's closer to work. Maybe I'll even be able to take some classes at night at CCNY."

"Over my dead body," was all my mother said, looking to Grandma for support.

"*Mameleh*," said Grandma, "nice girls don't leave home until they get married."

"You did," I whined. "You were only fourteen when you left the *shtetl* and moved to New York."

"So you're also running from the Cossacks?" my mother asked.

I looked at her with a nasty remark at the tip of my tongue but thought better of it and kept my mouth shut. I could defy my mother, but Grandma was my heart. The only thing less appealing than getting married was to continue living with my *meshuganah* family. I called my friend Howard.

I thought Howard was a good guy. I'd met him when I was fifteen and we moved onto the same block. We used to stand on the corner and sing doo-wop together. The whole senior year, Howard listened to me moan about Ralph. I'd lie with my head on his lap, and he'd stroke my hair and tell me how the guy was an ass and didn't deserve me. I knew that Howard had always wanted to stroke more than my hair, and, when I proposed marriage, he said yes. I was eighteen; he was twenty.

We had more harmony singing doo-wop together than we had as a couple. *The Ladies Home Journal* said passion would come. I knew what passion felt like, and I wasn't so sure I wanted to wait. Phyllis told me that there was no room for Howard because I wasn't over Ralph.

"Call him," she urged.

"What am I supposed to say? 'I'm engaged to be married, but all I think about is you?'"

"Exactly," she answered.

I finally gave in and took her advice. It had been a couple years since I'd called his house, and this time Ralph came to the phone.

"I need to see you," I said. "I am about to get married, and I have to be sure I'm not making a mistake."

He said he'd meet me Thursday night in the lobby of the Hotel New Yorker.

I changed my outfit six times that morning. I would have kept changing, but I had to get to work. I knew to keep it simple, so I settled on a navy skirt, white, man-tailored blouse, and a pair of black pumps. The day at the office dragged like no other. I'd tried to be a little late for our rendezvous so I wouldn't be the one standing around in the lobby, but I came early and I *was* the one standing around—my eyes fixated on the revolving door. I must've watched a hundred people come through, carrying their luggage. Not one person was Ralph.

I hadn't forgotten how handsome he was, but I was still floored when I saw him. It was October, and he still had a summer tan. I'd never seen him in a suit before. Ralph looked like a man out of another time and place, a very tasteful and fashionable one. He worked in the rag business, too, but he looked like royalty. He wore a navy sport jacket with a yellow plaid vest and a pocket watch. *What am I going to do?* I thought. *I still love this guy.*

He gave me a big smile and a warm *hello.* He seemed glad to see me, but I couldn't tell how much.

"Where do you want to go?" he asked.

"To the rock?" I said teasingly.

"Okay," he said. "Why not? I've got my car."

"Really? But we're not dressed for the country."

"So what," he said. "Be adventurous."

My excitement soared. I made arrangements to stay over at a coworker's house, called my mother, and gave her an excuse. "Stuck in the office," I said. "Staying over at Dillys's house. Don't wait up," Ralph put his arm around me and led me to the car. I pictured us on the rock. I was still a virgin of sorts, doing the good girl thing, waiting until after we were married, but this time, when Ralph asked, I fully intended to lie.

On the drive, we talked about Phyllis and Shelly's breakup. He said Shelly was pretty upset. Phyllis told me that if Ralph asked I should tell him that she was upset too, even though she was dating up a storm. She wanted to see if Shelly would swallow his pride and call her again.

Ralph wanted to know everything about Century of Boston. What was their fall line like? Were they doing purples? Reds? What did I think of the designer?

"So why did you want to see me?" he finally asked.

"Oh," I said, "bridal jitters. Why did you agree to see me?"

"Curiosity," he said, smiling, "and I have some things to tell you, but they can wait until we get to the rock." This just fed my excitement. *Was he going to tell me how much he'd missed me? Was he so glad that I had called?*

In anticipation of our time at the rock, we were quiet for the rest of the drive. The radio played Margaret Whiting, Tony Bennett, and Sinatra, and Ralph hummed along. I drummed my fingers on the seat, wishing I could call Phyllis.

We parked the car off to the side of the road. Ralph took my hand and we started the climb. The October air was crisp. The reds and golds of the leaves reflected in the moonlight. It must have rained earlier in the day, because the path was soggy and slippery underfoot. My ankles kept turning in my pumps.

"Are you okay?" he asked.

"Fine. Fine," I lied.

By now I was even more convinced that he would tell me something wonderful; otherwise why would we be schlepping up this boggy trail?

When we got to the top. I took off my shoes and he helped me up onto the rock. The sky was a panorama of stars. I looked up at him and waited for a kiss, but nothing happened. He looked at me with a shy smile. I began to deflate like a balloon after the party.

"What did you want to tell me?" I whispered.

"Are you ready for this?" he asked with excitement.

"For what?"

"There are three things," he said. "First, I'm changing my name from Lifshitz to *Lauren*; second, I'm going to make a million dollars; and third, I'm getting engaged to Susie."

"Susie who?" I asked.

"You know Susie. Your prom queen."

The first two were easy to believe, but the third was unfathomable. A vision of her as Glinda the Good Witch flashed through my brain, and I wanted to stab her with that goddamn wand.

"Since when does the Bronx go to Brooklyn?" was all I could manage to say.

My decision was made: I came down off the mountain and married Howard. In 1971, I ran into Susie at the pediatrician's office. I was there with my little boy; she was there with her little girl. By then, Ralph Lauren had won the Coty award for best menswear designer. I told Susie, in case she hadn't seen his ads, that the female model he used looked just like her. Long hair. Freckled nose. No pretense. Susie said she and Ralph had indeed gotten engaged, but she'd broken it off. The little girl with the runny nose was not his kid. She said that every time he'd pick her up for a date, he'd rearrange her clothes and adjust her bobby socks.

"It made me crazy, so I told him to take a hike," she said.

So what if he fixed your bobby socks? I thought. That seemed like a lame reason to break it off. He could have dressed me however he wanted, or, even better, *undressed* me *when*ever he wanted.

Thoughts of Ralph never left me. The more famous he became, the harder it was to keep him out of my mind. His fashions were in every store, his portrait in every magazine. My love had faded, but the memories of the passion I'd felt with him had not. *The Ladies Home Journal* was wrong; after twelve years of marriage, the passion with Howard never came. Had it not been for that summer with Ralph Lifshitz, I might never have known the excitement I could feel with a man.

My Wedding (1961)

∽ a photo left out ∾ in the sun

It is three in the morning. I am sitting at the desk in the living room of our new apartment with only a desk lamp to light the playing cards. The cartons, still unpacked, are stacked around me, awaiting our attention. A painting of a sunset—a memory of a weekend together in Provincetown, Rhode Island—leans against the wall. The baby kicks in my belly. I rub the spot—sure it's a little foot. I wonder if the baby is getting too big for its space and actively looking for a way out.

Howard has locked me out of our bedroom. I knocked and banged on the door, asked for an explanation, asked if he needed help. I cried and asked him to please let me in.

"Go away," is all he says, a strange voice expressing a mood I can't name. We have only been married for three years, but I'm already worried that I have married a crazy man.

"Are you sick?" I ask. "You have one hour to open this door, and then I am going to call the police."

Silence.

"What am I supposed to do, Howard? I'm tired. Open the fucking door."

I go back to the desk, deal out the cards and methodically put heart on heart and spade on spade. I recall my mother playing solitaire into the wee hours while waiting for my father to come home from yet another night out. I'd lie in my bed, hearing the shuffle of the cards, the bang on the table to even the deck—the flick of the Zippo lighting one cigarette after another.

Maybe I should have seen this coming. Today Howard did what he used to do when he lived at home with his parents—compulsively climbed up and down the outside steps, entering the house, checking to be sure he'd shut the burner on the stove. I counted—twelve times he went up and down the steps before he was satisfied that the house was safe, and he was free to leave.

I'm thinking now that my life has always been filled with crazy people.

The police tell me Kings County Hospital has a psychiatrist who makes house calls.

"At four in the morning?" I ask.

"Particularly at four in the morning," the dispatcher says.

Do I call? Don't I call? I imagine the doctor coming to the door, and I'm embarrassed, as if, somehow, I have caused this debacle. I go into the kitchen and put the kettle on, thinking that I can calm myself with a cup of tea. By the time the whistle blows, I know what has to be done—I reach for the phone.

"Howard, a doctor is coming. A psychiatrist."

"When?"

I can tell he is right next to the door. I can see the shadow of his feet.

"They didn't say. As soon as he can come, he will be here. Why don't you let me in and then we can end this and both go to sleep."

"No," he says. I see his shadow move away from the door.

I am tired of solitaire. I imagine the roving shrink, sitting in his car somewhere in Brooklyn, hearing the cackle of a call on the intercom and revving the engine to rush to the scene. The baby, affected by my distress, is kicking hard. My lower back hurts. I pace the floor, weaving between the cartons. The one marked PHOTOGRAPHS grabs my attention.

At the top of the carton is a small plastic book with a white spiral binding containing Polaroids of our wedding taken by my maid of honor, Phyllis—helping us out, saving us money by being our photographer. I will discover in the years to come that Polaroid pictures fade with age, but this night, only three years into our married life, the photos, like the memories, are still sharp. I begin leafing through the pictures, trying to distract myself while waiting for the doctor.

The cover of the album says, "December 24, 1961: our Emily Post Wedding."

The first picture that came to mind was in my memory, not the album. It had snowed the night before. I recall hiking up the train of my gown and holding my pumps in my hand— better to have frozen feet then ruin the shoes—and climbing over the mound of snow that blocked the path to the door of the temple.

In the photos, I am wearing a white satin gown. The bejeweled bodice dips to a point at the waist, and the skirt fans out into a long train. On my head is a pearl crown meant to give a queenly touch, but, when removed, it left little red puncture wounds like a crown of thorns across my brow.

The inspiration for my royal wedding was a single weekend at my friend Dillys's apartment. Dillys, a coworker at Century of Boston, was smart and soft-spoken and the only one of our office staff able to keep our boss and the owner's son in check. Alan the Arrogant, as we called him, was a pain in the ass, but Dillys managed him with such charm and self-assurance that he was oblivious to her manipulations.

Because we were all crammed into Grandma's apartment, I was delighted when Dillys invited me to spend the weekend with her. Her husband, Peter, was off training with the ROTC—I had no idea what the ROTC was. I asked; she explained, but it didn't stick, and it became a subject to ignore.

Dillys and Peter lived on the second floor of a brownstone in another part of Brooklyn known as the Heights. The neighborhood was so different from Brownsville that it was like a different city. The tree-lined streets were clean and open. I was most impressed by the quiet. It was five thirty in the evening on a warm fall day, and there were no children playing stickball on the street, and no mothers screaming out the window, calling them in for dinner.

Walking into Dillys's apartment was like walking onto the set of *The Philadelphia Story*. It had a gracious simplicity, seemingly achieved without effort—the sleek lines of a Maurice Villency Danish teakwood dining room table and chairs, two sterling silver candlesticks, each with a tapered beeswax candle, flanking a crystal bowl. Dillys served me wine out of Waterford glasses and dinner on gold-rimmed Lenox china. Her *tchotchkes*, as my mother would unwittingly call them, were spare—not ceramic mementoes from Coney Island outings, but Steuben glass animals and fruit neatly placed on the sideboard. Dillys's family pictures were not tin-typed and faded, or headshots taken in a photo booth, but painted portraits hung on the living room wall. I slept between monogrammed sheets and awoke to WQXR playing classical music, but what I found to be most impressive were the floor-to-ceiling shelves lined with books. Had Dillys read all these books, or was Peter the reader? I asked, but she just smiled.

Dillys was happy to play Pygmalion, educating the underclass. Had I known the word, I would have labeled my behavior and all the questions I asked *gauche*, but my concern for showing my ignorance was less important than learning the names of all that I saw.

In the same way I studied Dillys' apartment, I studied her manner and her dress. Later in my life, I would decide that her style was actually *no* style—a generic distillation that said little about the individual—but back then, I thought shirtwaist dresses, scarves carefully tied at the neck, and little gold butterflies pinned on the shoulder of cashmere sweater sets were exactly the look to achieve. If I saved, I could afford the sweater set, but the pin was out of reach.

Why was I so ready to cast aside the richness of my Jewish heritage? Why was I such a WASP wannabe, glomming on to snobbery and its affectations? Maybe I got it from my father, as he, more than my mother, aspired to rise in class, but he didn't quite know how to get there. He spent money he didn't have on suits and monogrammed shirts—his star sapphire ring did not come with a diploma and was a dead giveaway.

I put the pictures back in the carton and try one more time to get Howard to open the door.

"Howard. Are you sleeping?"

"Go away," he says.

"Are you crying? You sound as if you are crying."

"Go away," he says, his tone turning cold.

Only fifteen minutes after calling the hospital, I begin to feel desperate—now, without question, I want him here. If he hasn't come by four thirty, I will call again. I go back to the box of photographs.

There are a bunch of pictures from high school, but only one with Howard. He is sitting on the stoop of his house, a cigarette between his fingers. He's seventeen, but he could be taken for forty. Was it his looks or his demeanor that belied his age? In the picture, he is looking up at the photographer and biting his lip, an angry expression I have come to know well.

My father changed our name from Meyerowitz to Meyers. Ralph, when we dated, announced he was changing his name from Lifshitz to Lauren. Young, urban Jews were fixated on everything WASP. Ralph knew, and I knew, that he would get rich catering to these desires. Girls would do anything to look like *a shiksa*. In 1958, girls would disappear at the end of junior year in high school and reemerge in September looking like Gidget with perky little noses that had as much business on their faces as my friend Phyllis's painted-on eyebrows. Different doctors had signature noses. You could tell the doctor by the nose. It didn't seem to matter if it fit the girl's face—it was the only nose he did. In the end, nose or no nose, you could always tell a Jewish girl by her mother and her mother's investment in having a *shiksa* daughter.

My friend Dillys had class—that one visit to her apartment, and I was stamped with the Protestant imprimatur. I asked Dillys for help planning my wedding. She advised me to get a copy of Emily Post's *Etiquette*. I had bought the myth that one could escape her crazy Jewish family by learning how to make a soufflé and serving it on the right dishes.

It was imperative that the wedding be "Emily Post" perfect. I sent out the *correct* wedding invitations, replaced Uncle Seymour and his clarinet with a young man and his cello. There was no chopped liver or pickled herring at the smorgasbord—actually, there was no smorgasbord. Instead, I'd enlisted a few waiters to walk around with trays of finger sandwiches. The large floral centerpieces, usually sent home with the lucky guest who had a little note under their plate, were replaced by a single rose at each setting. I gave myself credit, not only for meeting the measure of the book, but for managing to do it on a shoestring, as my father was still having a *situation*. There had been no money for college and now there was no money for a wedding.

My father, to his credit, saw the glaring fly in the ointment—I had picked the wrong man to play the groom. He took me aside and tried to talk sense into me, "You can do better," he said. "What's your rush? You're only nineteen. What's your hurry?"

I couldn't tell if his conviction was out of concern for me, or if I was letting him down by my choice, but my bags were packed, the pillbox hat was in its box, the white gloves with the pearl buttons at the wrists were laid next to the Chanel-like suit—there was no way I was canceling this trip.

I knew in my heart that my father was right and that Howard was a mistake, but desperation and obfuscation feed each other—I needed a way out, and so did Howard. His fights with me were nothing compared to his rages against his smothering mother. When I tried to instruct him on how to behave in the world, he understandably balked—I was his mother all over again. The more I pushed, the worse it got. I had too much riding on the fantasy to be interrupted by the facts—my desires weren't his. He was too uncomfortable in the world to which I aspired. Brooklyn is his home. This apartment around the corner from his parents is his refuge. So why the hell is he locked in the bedroom?

Where the hell is that doctor? I am so tired. I look—the light is still on but there is no shadow at the door.

Howard himself was not beyond pretense. I say this as part of my Emily Post defense—Howard also had his fantasies. Throughout high school, he tried, as did many of the adolescent boys at the time, to affect the Elvis Presley-James Dean look—not easy given that he was a chubby teenager with a soft face and ruddy complexion. Despite the heavy application of grease and continuous combing, he could not get his thin blonde hair to stay in the duck's ass style of the day. The leather jacket and motorcycle boots didn't do it either, as he had no hips and a flat ass—it's hard to look cool when you have to keep hiking up your jeans. There was poignancy to his efforts, because though he tried mightily, they just weren't working.

My high school years were unsuccessful as well. We had moved the beginning of sophomore year, and once again I was the new kid on the block—new school, new rules. I longed for the freedom to try on different identities and new behaviors, but the precariousness of my parents' marriage told me that my mother was too fragile to handle a rebellious daughter I did manage to do some dating. In the beginning of my junior year I dated Joe. He was a tall, good-looking guy with a great smile and a strong body. He wore white-collared shirts, open at the neck, sleeves rolled up, and tight blue jeans. He was poor, but we still managed to have great dates—riding back and forth on the Staten Island Ferry for a nickel or hanging out in Prospect Park for nothing. I think I might have had sex with Joe, except whenever we kissed, my mother's admonitions rang in my ear. *They won't respect you in the morning* and *Why should they buy the cow if they can get the milk for free?* she'd say. I believed I had no choice but to be a *good girl* And, as I've written, college never happened. Until the I'd-rather-not-talk-about-it wedding night, my good girl status, like my hymen, remained intact.

I suppose you could say that Howard and I both failed adolescence, but young adulthood was not looking too promising either. We decided to do what many virginal, non-college-bound kids did back then—get married and play grownup.

When I proposed marriage, he grabbed it—the details of how we would support ourselves would come later. However, during the short year of our engagement, Howard continued to have royal fights with his mother. He would scream, get red in the face, and jump around the house like a caged tiger. His rages should have been a warning, but, as I've said, I couldn't let reality interfere with fantasy.

I believe the wedding, despite the pretense, was a success, but the honeymoon was a disaster. Sex was awkward and painful, but in truth, hadn't I set Howard up to fail? It wasn't his fault that I felt no passion. It wasn't that I lacked the capacity for erotic arousal; I'd found that out in my brief summer romance with Ralph. It was just that I lacked it with him. To make the honeymoon even more of a disappointment, as we were walking on the beach, I looked up, and there was my ex-boyfriend Joe. I hadn't seen him in a year. He introduced me to his new wife, Claudia. They were having their honeymoon at *our* hotel. Joe looked great! Claudia looked great! I've no idea how I looked—down at the mouth, I suspect. I was wearing a new bathing suit that had only marginally passed the Howard test—his insistence that before I left the room, I move my body in contorted ways to be sure that there was no hint of a breast or cleavage. When I ran into Joe, my breasts were as flat as my mood. I gave him a hug—not too tight lest Howard erupt—took my leave, went back to my room, and cried. One week after the wedding, and the fantasy had faded like a photo left out in the sun.

At last there is a knock at the door—a young man not much older than I stands there with a doctor's case in hand. I usher him in and tell him what I can about the situation. Three hours have passed since we got home, and I still have no idea why Howard is locked in the bedroom.

"Seven months pregnant," I say when he looks at my belly.

He tries to reassure me that he will take care of it, but given that neither of us has any idea what *it* is, I am not reassured. Howard lets him into the bedroom, and I go back to nervously playing solitaire.

Forty-five minutes later he comes out.

"You can go to bed now. I gave him a shot of valium, and here's a prescription to fill in the morning. I also suggest he see a psychiatrist. He's going to sleep."

"Yes, thank you, but what was happening?"

The doctor looks at me and then looks away. "I have another call. I need to go," he says.

"You can't go. What was going on?"

"I can't say; patient-client privilege."

"I don't give a damn. You can't leave me here and not tell me what was going on." I rubbed my belly for sympathy.

"All right," he says, sitting down. "Your husband was having fantasies."

"What fantasies?"

"He was having fantasies of wanting to kill you, but it's okay. They were only fantasies. They scared him, so he locked you out of the bedroom so he wouldn't hurt you."

"My husband wants to kill me and you are *leaving*?"

"I told you, he is sleeping now. I believe they were passing thoughts and will be gone by morning. Go to bed. Get some sleep."

The doctor leaves. I don't know how I can stand to get in bed with that man. *Would the shot wear off during the night? Would he wake up and kill me in my sleep?* I clean up the cards and put them back in the desk. I wash my teacup. I put the wedding pictures back in the carton and decide that I am too tired to care anymore. The whole night has been a badly written mystery and I no longer care about the ending. I slide under the sheets, careful not to touch him.

The next morning Howard wakes. I try again to ask what happened the night before—what set him off—but he looks at me and scowls, as if I am prying and insensitive to his anguish.

"It's over. Don't think about it. Let it go," he says. "I'm going to my mother's. I'll be back later."

"Aren't you going to help me unpack?"

"Later," he says.

Howard was right, it *was* over. It took twelve years and one thousand *fuck you* and *fuck you too*, three kids, and a family disaster before I would admit to myself that by marrying Howard, I hadn't escaped the family tell. I'd only climbed down deeper.

dr. zhivago

Grandma took me to Orchard Street, on the Lower East Side of Manhattan, to buy the layette. I wanted to tell her about the experience with Howard and the psychiatrist, but I knew it would upset her. She would have no context in which to understand it, so I kept it to myself and tried not to let it ruin the day.

"This is where I lived when I got off the boat," Grandma said, pointing to a tenement to the left. "The street was like it is now. Maybe a little more crowded."

It was hard to imagine it more crowded, as it was bustling with peddlers. Wares on wagons. Small shops with dusty windows squeezed together. Pages from the *Jewish Daily Forward* swirling around my feet. Horses swishing flies with their tails. We passed a butcher shop with a sign in Hebrew promising that it was kosher. On one of the wagons, I spotted orange bloomers and corseted bras.

"This is where I shop. Where else would I get the bloomers?" Grandma said.

I had to agree with her. I'd never seen corseted bras and orange bloomers in the department store.

Grandma led me into a shop so small that it looked like a room in a dollhouse. A little gray-haired lady, slightly stooped, her hair pinned back in a neat knot, smiled hello.

"This is my granddaughter. My first great-grandchild," Grandma said in Yiddish, pointing at my belly. "We need a layette. It should be in yellow."

"Yellow, but maybe some blue," I said.

"Blue, *mameleh*? You want it should be a boy but you don't know it's a boy?"

Grandma held up little onesies, bibs, booties and soft little hats with cat's ears and debated the price of each item. The gray-haired lady didn't seem to mind. When we were done, both she and Grandma looked satisfied—a beautiful yellow layette with one token blue blanket awaited my baby.

Everything was done. The baby's room was papered. The crib was assembled. The dressing table was in place. I had painted an unfinished rocker shiny white. It would be perfect for nursing.

"Why are you going to nurse? Who nurses in this day and age? Even I didn't nurse. Take it from your mother, there is no reason. It's primitive," my mother said.

"Grandma thinks it's best for the baby."

"Grandma is out of date."

"Dr. Spock thinks it's best for the baby."

"It wasn't enough I had to put up with Emily Post for the wedding? Now I have to put up with Dr. Spock for the baby."

"It's not your baby, Ma, it's my baby."

"Fine, be that way until you need my help. Then it will be, 'Ma, can you please come and take the baby,' and I'll say, 'Okay, but leave me your breast.'"

Howard got a job working for my father, who got his job working for his brother-in-law Harry. Uncle Harry was the big boss. Harry wasn't happy that he had to rescue my father. My father wasn't happy that he was no longer his own boss and had to work for Harry. Howard wasn't happy, because working for his father-in-law meant that he couldn't get his own job, which was the truth. No one was happy, and I wasn't happy either because by then it was October 22—one month past my due date—and the baby still hadn't come.

November 8, 1964, my twenty-second birthday. I got through the last week by telling myself that the baby was waiting to give me the best birthday present ever. When midnight came and went, I began to cry. Was it possible I'd never give birth? Howard was sleeping. The living room was dark. I was standing at the window staring down at the street—crying in frustration and deep disappointment. I had decided that the baby had rejected me. He didn't want to live in Brooklyn around the corner from his grandparents. He didn't want a father who dreamt of killing his mother. I imagined him retreating to an embryo and then an ovum. I was lost in this grotesque fantasy when my water broke.

The doctor's on-call service told us to wait until the contractions were ten minutes apart before coming to the hospital.

Howard said, "Let's go now."

"They said to wait."

"I don't care what they said, let's go. We've already waited six weeks too long. Get in the car. Let's go."

I could tell that Howard was frantic as I moaned with each pain. He wanted his job over with. Once he'd delivered me to the hospital, his job would be done. He was ready for the hand off.

Admitting said we were too early and left us sitting in the waiting room until my mother walked in and raised holy hell.

"Why did you call my mother?" I hissed at Howard.

"Because she told me to."

"I told you not to. That I wanted to do this without her."

"She's your mother, Linda; she belongs here."

When the next contraction came, I let out a groan that was not commensurate with the pain.

Had I known what to expect, I would have rooted for the waiting room. The labor room was a small, rectangular room, with one light and a very small window up near the ceiling. For the next twenty-one hours, I stared at the cracks in the ceiling. A nurse with wide hips and a large Afro gave me an enema and shaved my pubic hair—then settled me in bed, put the railings up, and left. Periodically she would come in, look between my legs, shake her head, and pat my hand, as if, despite my efforts, I still hadn't passed the entrance exam and, therefore, wasn't ready for the big test. She assured me that the doctor would come when I was closer to delivery.

"Then I want to see my husband."

"No one's allowed in the labor room. Husbands are not allowed in the labor room," she said.

By the eighteenth hour, a new nurse had come on shift. She took pity and let Howard come up. "Fifteen minutes. That's it, fifteen minutes." Howard had to lean against the wall to allow her to pass.

Howard, in an attempt to distract me, told me the husbands in the waiting room had a pool, and the first one to become a father would win the pot.

I screamed through the next contraction, no longer caring about being a disturbance.

"How many pots?" I cried.

"Four," he whispered.

I'm sorry you're a loser," I said

"Your mother wants to come up."

"Is she in on the pool?"

"No. She's just pacing and smoking and muttering that you are an ungrateful daughter because you won't let her up."

"Tell her I'm sorry, but—" And here another strong contraction came and took the words right out of my mouth.

David was born on November 9. He was beautiful. I was elated. Howard was elated. My parents were elated.

"He has red hair. Who has red hair?" said my mother-in-law. "You have brown hair. Howard has blonde hair. Nobody has red hair."

I had a dream from the time I was a little girl that I would have three children. Having spent my childhood alone in my room pulling a yoyo by its string and saying, "Nice doggy," I was determined that my baby would not suffer the loneliness of being an only child. I spent the next seven years pregnant or nursing. My second son, Jonathan, was born on March 16, 1967. He had ABO blood incompatibility. That meant that my blood and his blood were incompatible. I'd hoped that just meant his blood and not our personalities, but concerns for his survival trumped any other thoughts. A special doctor was called in, a tall David Niven lookalike with all the pomp. He arrived with six or seven eager young doctors in tow. They circled my bed, smiled wanly, and then pinned all their attention on him. As I lay on the bed, my lip quivering, fearful for my baby and worried that I might be going to a funeral rather than a bris, the doctor announced with absolutely no humility that he was the "font," and that I was fortunate that he was going to be the doctor taking care of my baby. I didn't know if he was strutting to give me confidence or if he really walked that way.

"Your baby failed the APGAR test. His bilirubin is going up as we speak. He needs to have his blood exchanged."

"With what?"

"Donor blood. O positive blood." He seemed annoyed that he had to state the obvious. "Fortunately, I'm available, and I will do it this afternoon. One cc in and one cc out. It will take several hours, but after the procedure is complete, he will be fine."

I stared at Howard. He shook his head and shrugged his shoulders.

"Tell the nurse to bring me my baby. I want to see my baby before they drain his blood."

The nurse brought Jonathan to me. His skin was the color of saffron. His little body stiffened when I tried to hold him. His legs were taut and his toes splayed. I couldn't cuddle him. He would have none of it, as if he knew what he was about to face. The nurse took him. She gave me a gentle smile. I knew she understood how frightened I was.

"I'm sorry, baby," I cried. "I'm sorry we were not compatible. I promise I will make it up to you. You can nurse until you are two or until you go to school. Whatever you want. You sweet little boy."

That would turn out to be a false promise because, fearful that even my milk was tainted with antibodies, I would not be allowed to nurse at all.

Dr. Font turned out to be a wizard. Within twenty-four hours, Jonathan's skin turned pink, his hair turned red, he passed the APGAR, and I was allowed to take him home.

"Looks like my Morris, only my Morris doesn't have red hair," my mother-in-law said.

On January 13, 1970, my third son, Robert, was born with red hair and blood incompatibility. The treatment protocol had changed since Jonathan's birth. They no longer exchanged the baby's blood. Instead, they put him in an incubator under fluorescent lights. Robert stayed under the lights for eight days. Mothers had to put on sterile gowns and masks. The nurse would wheel the bassinette up to the window, and I would get to see my baby. I was not allowed to touch him. He couldn't hear me through the glass, so I couldn't sing to him. For eight days, I pumped my breasts, waiting to get him home, hold him in my arms, and feed him. By then doctors had decided it was safe to nurse, so even my mother stopped complaining that I was breastfeeding. However, my mother-in-law didn't stop whispering that there must be another man because her son didn't have red hair. Shortly thereafter Howard grew a beard. It was red. My mother-in-law finally shut up, although I was too busy to care. I was twenty-seven years old, and I had three children under the age of five. I was overworked and certainly underpaid. I'd looked around at some of my friends whose husbands, actively and happily, shared in childcare, and I knew that it wasn't hair color that defined paternity.

The kids were great little guys. I loved them. I loved the hugs, the smushy kisses, the smell of their little bodies after a bath. I loved watching Sesame Street and reading books together—but it wasn't enough. It was supposed to be enough, but it wasn't. There must have been something wrong with me, or it would have been enough. Maybe if I'd liked being a wife? Maybe if I'd liked being Howard's wife? What if going to the supermarket with two kids in the cart and one holding my hand was fun and not an exercise in courage? What if the fourth dinner of the week was salami and eggs, and it counted as a real dinner instead of a cop-out meal? What if I made a needlepoint that said HOME SWEET HOME over the picture of a house with a little red chimney instead of the one I designed that said FUCK HOUSEWORK in Roman letters over a broken broom? What if I could go to college at night and get a *real* job, one that paid a salary instead of a clothing allowance? Maybe then I would be a good enough mom. Howard and I fought. We fought all the time. He felt the weight of my disappointment. He knew he wasn't living up to my expectations, but I don't think he was living up to his own either.

When the kids got sick, and I couldn't get out of the house, life became unbearable. One fall each of the kids got chicken pox consecutively. I'd been in the house for three weeks straight. I no longer bothered to get dressed in the morning. I'd been up during the night changing diapers. Giving meds. Begging them not to scratch their scabs. Kissing their foreheads. By the time Sunday came, I was ready for a padded cell or a great escape.

I fed them breakfast. Then I went into the bedroom and put on a pair of jeans and a sweatshirt. A little makeup and lipstick. Came out and announced to Howard that I was going to the movies.

"You're going out. I worked all week and now I'm supposed to babysit?"

"Babysit? They're your kids."

"You're not going to the movies. Women don't go alone to the movies."

"Says who?"

"Says me."

I walked out the door. I felt frightened and exhilarated. I was the teenage girl escaping out her bedroom window to meet her date. My date was *Dr. Zhivago*, Omar Sharif. It was a three hour and twenty-minute film, the longest I could find. I looked around and didn't see any single women, but I didn't care. I didn't need a man to go to a movie. I loved every snowy moment of that film. When I got home, I got big hugs from the kids and silence from Howard. I went into the kitchen, made salami and eggs, and served them with a smile.

⌒ had i won at bingo ⌒

The church in Brooklyn was not near my mother's apartment. She had to take two buses to get there. She said she didn't mind—it was worth it. It was August 1970. It was hot and humid outside, but when I walked into the church, it was cool and cavernous with an unfamiliar smell of incense. I don't know where the pews had gone, but they had been replaced by long aluminum tables that wound through the hall like metal scales on a silver snake. There might have been a hundred tables in the room and eight or ten times as many chairs, all facing the altar. Perched on the altar was a large glass canister filled with balls. Next to the canister was a microphone. No one was at the microphone.

Earlier, we'd been part of the throng of people gathered on the steps of the church, waiting for the carved wooden doors to open. At exactly 1:00 p.m. the doors majestically parted, and a stampede of women pushed their way in like they were trying to get to the sales tables at S, Kline's department store. They should have shopped before they came, because mostly they were a sorry lot. They came in housecoats, some with stockings rolled to the ankles. They had unkempt gray hair, held in place by bobby pins. Resignation lined their faces. Other women were *oysgeputst*, over-dressed, with too much rouge and too-red lips. A few reluctant husbands straggled along behind.

My mother, as always, was dressed appropriately. She wore flowered capri pants, an orange belt tightened over her small potbelly, and a white nylon shirt. Her hair, colored and set each week by Andrea the hairdresser, was neatly combed into a beehive. She had worn wire-rimmed glasses for the twenty-seven years I had known her, but had recently traded them in for a new pair—yellow to match her hair, and shaped like butterfly wings, with rhinestones on the temples.

My mother, at fifty-two, could still be called an attractive woman, but her looks were dictated by her mood. When she was angry, she gritted her teeth, her eyes flashed, and her chin stuck out in defiance. She had a hard look like a tough girl who had grown up in a bad neighborhood. When she was sad, her eyes looked inward, her features disappearing into her face, her determination gone—she became invisible. But my mother also had a lively, fun-loving side. She would listen to Cab Calloway singing "Minnie the Moocher," dance around the living room, and recount the days she had danced in the marathons.

"Your father and I were hot on the dance floor," she bragged. "We could do a mean Lindy Hop. He'd throw me over his head and between his legs. We were something. . . ." Her voice would trail off as her face lit up with the memory, and then, as if by a switch, the smile would go dim.

She was twenty-three when she married my father. In their wedding pictures, she looks triumphant. Grandma told me the bridal gown had been rented. "That's what they used to do back then," she said.

To Grandma, for whom there was no part of a chicken that couldn't be eaten, turned into soup, or stuffed into cabbage, the idea of renting, rather than buying a wedding gown made perfect sense.

"What you supposed to do when the wedding is over?" she'd ask. "You should pay good money to storage so they should stick it in a freezer? You should pack it in a trunk with mothballs? You should think that maybe your daughter or future daughter-in-law wants not to be her own self on her wedding day but instead she should walk down the aisle looking like you . . . *Meshugeh*, the dress is just for a day—it's the marriage that's forever."

I, on the other hand, was disappointed that the dress was gone. I loved that gown in the photo. I would have worn it when I got married, would have been happy to look like my mother. I wanted to feel as I imagined she felt before the disappointment and the bitterness set in.

Inside the church, my mother warned me of this woman or that, who might steal our seats. These were not assigned seats, but they had been spoken for by repetitive use. My mother had appointed herself to the fifth table from the front and the fifth seat to the center. She insisted that was her lucky seat. She held me by the arm, pulling me behind her, yelling over her shoulder that when we got to the table I should sit on her right-hand side.

I am eight again. She is dragging me across the green courtyard of our garden apartment complex, screaming something about what I did or didn't do, or what I should or shouldn't have done. I can't hear her over my own wails except when she yells at me to shut up or she'd give me something to cry about.

"Just wait till I get you inside," she warns.

I know I'm in for it. It has happened too many times before—no trial, no defense. Just punishment.

It seems that I have embarrassed her by not wanting to play with her friend's daughter. The mother complained to my mother. Her friend's daughter is an idiot girl who wouldn't share anything. I hated her. I try to explain to my mother that this is not a girl I should befriend, but she can't hear me. She is yelling for all the neighbors to hear—they shouldn't think that she did not have control over her daughter: "You are a mean, selfish ingrate of a child."

When we make it into the apartment, she throws me down against the steps and, in a frenzy, beats my head, my arms, wherever her hands land. I know that this is no longer about playing with the idiot kid, it is about my father's never coming home for dinner. I decide that enough is enough. I will myself not to cry. For a moment she hits me harder, and then, as if defeated, her hands drop to her side and the beating stops.

"Do you feel better now?" I ask.

She never hits me again.

There in the bingo church, I wrestled my wrist from her grasp.

"What is the matter with you?" I asked. I was hot and annoyed. "What does it matter where we sit?"

She looked at me as if I didn't understand. She was right. I didn't understand this whole bingo thing. I knew she went four, sometimes five times a week. She'd bribed me to go with her, offering to pay for a sitter, buy dinner for my family, and take me to the beauty parlor—anything as long as I'd go with her. But bingo was not my idea of a day off. Taking care of three little kids, to me an afternoon off would have been the opportunity to take a nap without the children at home, or to go grocery shopping without two kids in the cart and one on my hip.

I had finally given in because I was tired of the harangue, and I also wanted to make her happy. I had always wanted to make her happy. There were times I succeeded—once, I recall, when I let her teach me the rumba and then again when I had agreed to go to the high school senior prom with that kid Elliot—the first, learning the rumba, was a gift I cherished, the second was a sacrifice. My mother never went to the senior prom at Thomas Jefferson High School because she, like my father, had quit when she turned sixteen.

"You shouldn't miss this opportunity," she insisted. "You'll be sorry for the rest of your life."

It hardly seemed possible that I would ever regret not going to the senior prom with Elliot, but I saw it meant a lot to her, and also to my friend Phyllis, so I went.

"We have to hurry or *that* one will take my seat." She pointed with her head.

"Which one is *that* one?" I asked, like it mattered.

"The one with the *farbissener pisk*, the sourpuss."

I looked over and saw whom she meant. This short, fierce lady with slightly bowed legs and a face that looked like she'd been sucking a lemon was elbowing her way to the front. My mother, realizing I couldn't move fast enough, dropped my wrist and beat her to the chair. She plunked down her purse on the chair next to her and waited for me to catch up. By the time I got there, I felt like I had run a marathon. I plopped into the chair. Out of the corner of my eye, I watched as my mother furtively started pulling something out of her purse. It was a small rubber troll with flyaway orange hair.

"What is that? What are you doing with that? Isn't that the toy you gave to David?" I asked. My son David was five. He was already a collector of strange objects, and he liked that troll. "Did he give it back to you?"

"He won't miss it," she said. "I'll get him another one. Why are you looking at me? I said I'd get him another one!" Whenever my mother felt guilty, she got adamant.

"That isn't even the point. Why is it here?" Then I looked around and I saw that many of the women were doing the same thing, pulling these weird objects out of their purses and setting them up like talismans before a shrine.

"It's my lucky charm," she explained. "I'm a big winner here. Three times I won the jackpot. Five hundred dollars a shot, and I didn't even have to split it. Everybody hates me," she said. "Do I give a damn? Let them hate me. I'm the winner. It's worth it."

I began to understand the lure of the bingo parlor. A parlor in a church is where the monastic are allowed to speak. It was there in that church that my mother, silenced by my father, had found a voice. I looked around, and I saw that she was being eyed and envied. For two and a half hours a day, four days a week—she mattered. It was less about the money and more about accruing the envy. I didn't know what to say to her—*I'm glad you win. It's nice to be a winner.* Anything I'd said would have been a lie, because what I really wanted to say was, *I'm sorry. I'm sorry you have to come here at all.*

Ushers came around the room selling lapboards. Each board held two bingo cards—my mother bought twelve. She took ten and gave me two.

"That's quite an investment," I chided.

"Not really, I sometimes play fifteen. You want more? Here take another two."

I told her two was enough. "Where are your discs to cover the numbers?"

"I don't use any."

I was stunned. "How do you keep track?"

"Your mother's a smart lady," she answered. "Go tell that to your father."

I ignored the dig at my father. "I know you're smart, but still you're going to play . . ."

A hush came over the room as a priest took the podium.

I thought he was going to bless the proceedings. I turned to ask my mother, but she shushed me.

He mumbled a few words then reached into the basket. There was a tension in the room as he was about to drop the first ball.

"B-4," he called. "B-4," he repeated. My mother looked down at her board and eyeballed her *B*s to see if she had any fours. She looked over at my boards.

"You don't have any," she stated.

"I can see that. Are you going to play my boards too?" I was beginning to get into it.

"Don't get testy with me. You haven't played before."

"It's bingo, Mom," I said. "It's not rocket science."

"B-2," called the priest. "B-2."

And so went the afternoon—two and a half hours of bingo. My mother won about one hundred dollars. I still didn't understand how she had done it without the discs, but she sure knew when she won. She stood up and waved madly until she was seen, and then she would sit down, self-satisfied, look around at all the losers, and wait for the usher to bring her booty. Only once did she have to share the pot with the woman who sucked lemons. My mother shrugged. "I'll let her have a few. She shouldn't think I don't care," she said, laughing.

As we filed out of the church, we were hit again by the late summer heat.

"Come on." my mother said. "I'll blow you to a soda. It's right around the corner."

"No, Ma. I can't." I told her. "I've got to get back."

She knew I wasn't just leaving—I was escaping. I'd had enough. There was something about the whole afternoon that made me terribly sad. It was more like a cult gathering than an afternoon's distraction. My mother's emotional pain was contagious. I knew that my father was close to leaving her again—they were killing each other. I thought that he stood a chance at happiness without her. I hoped, beyond hope, that she would find some too. She was only fifty-two years old—young enough to start a new life. Meanwhile, my own marriage was in shambles.

My father kept calling me. "You've got to talk to your mother. She's driving me crazy." She kept calling me and crying that she'd been a saint, but he was killing her. I'd had it. *Enough.* Even if she didn't want out from under, I did.

We were standing on the steps of the church.

"Do you think . . . ?" she started to ask, and I knew what was coming. "Your father . . . what do you think? I'm asking you, Linda, what do you think? I'm telling you he has somebody. He doesn't come home till late. Every night. . . two, three in the morning. What does he tell you? You must know," she said.

"I'm sorry, Mom. I don't know why you think he talks to me."

"You're the only one he talks to except maybe his sister. He'll listen to you. Tell him to cut it out once and for all and be a husband. If he has to live a lie, so let him live a lie. Tell him," she pleaded. "You at least owe me that."

"Mom, please," I begged. "Give me a break."

"What am I asking?" Her eyes got dark. "I'm only asking you to do what a good daughter should do—help her mother."

Monkey in the middle, I thought.

"I've got to go . . . the kids. But thanks for the afternoon. It was really fun," I lied.

"Here," she said, resigned, "take a cab. Don't take a bus. You're tired. It's too hot."

I accepted the cash, even knowing it came with a dose of guilt. I was tired, and I was sad. Had I won at bingo, I would have paid my own way home.

I left my mother standing on the steps of the church.

Parent's Wedding

∽ dead serious ∾

The first time my mother tried to kill herself, I wasn't even born. It was when my father broke off their engagement and ran off with Eva Mike, the *shiksa*. Her attempt succeeded in lassoing him in, and the wedding went ahead as planned. They walked down the aisle, made their vows, and broke the glass. According to my mother, *her* wedding was perfect.

"If you don't believe me," she'd say, "then look at the pictures. Your father couldn't have been happier."

My father looks directly into the camera with the expression of a man who knows he is handsome. My mother, thin like a model, blonde hair swept up in the fashion of the day—is beautiful. Her smile is not forced. Her eyes are not desperate. Her rented, white, satin gown with the pointed coller, cinched waist is elegant. It had sleeves like an artist's smock, tight at the wrist with wide cuffs. In one picture, the long train swirls around her feet like icing at the bottom of a cake, and resting there on the train is a large bouquet of white calla lilies, the symbol of purity, of union, and of death.

The pictures were perfect, but the marriage was not. Six years later, my father took off with Lillian, the secretary. My mother, having promised *until death do us part*, made a second suicide attempt.

I hadn't learned about those earlier attempts until years later, after I was married to Howard. It was December 31, 1962. We had just celebrated our first wedding anniversary, and we were getting dressed to go to a New Year's Eve party when there was a knock at the door. My mother was standing there, holding a suitcase.

"I just wanted to say goodbye," she said. "I'm on my way to a hotel to jump out the window."

She said this without inflection, as if she'd come to tell me she was going to throw out a favorite dress because it no longer fit. I stood at the door and stared at her. Howard, having heard what she said, moved me aside and invited her in. She sat down at the dining room table and started to cry. I sat at the other end of the room behind the desk, feet up, arms embracing my knees, looking up at the ceiling.

"Your father has left me. I'm going to a hotel to jump out the window. That's it, Linda, I've had it. I've been a saint, a saint," she said, "but enough is enough."

The importance of what she was saying didn't register, or maybe it hit a pocket of pain that I could only manage with black humor, but I wondered aloud what the point of the suitcase was.

"Do you have a reservation at a hotel?" I asked. "It's New Year's Eve. If you don't have a reservation, then forget it. You can't jump out the window without a reservation."

Howard leaned down and whispered, "What's the matter with you? Look at her," he said. "Go put your arm around her."

He was right, I should go give her a hug, but I couldn't

move. I just sat and stared at her. I felt guilty, angry, helpless, but I didn't feel loving.

Aunt Laura called to see if my mother was with me. She must have spoken to her earlier in the day. In cryptic bursts, she told me about my mother's earlier attempts. The memory from first grade and the meaning of the message I was to give my father suddenly registered—and the realization that she would have left me when I was just a little kid hit hard. I didn't know what to say.

"Don't let her leave," Aunt Laura said.

"Okay," I muttered and hung up the phone.

"Who was that?" my mother asked.

"Aunt Laura. She wanted to know if you were here and if you were all right."

"Yeah, I'm just *fine*. Did she say anything about your father?"

"No. She just wanted to know about you."

"He's probably right there in her house. She's protecting him. She always protected him."

"He's her brother, Ma. What do you expect?"

"What I expect is that someone should stick up for me. You should stick up for me. Tell your father to come home, take care of his wife—be a *mensch*."

It took several hours before my mother calmed down. She agreed to let Howard drive her home, but only if I once again promised to plead her case to my father.

"Tell him your mother's a saint for putting up with him," she said. "Tell him he should kiss the ground I walk on."

This was a litany I'd heard many times.

"Dad, Mom wants you to come home and kiss the ground she walks on," I'd say.

"Yeah? Well, you can tell your mother I ain't kissing no ground. She's crazy but she's your mother. I'm not going to say anything bad about your mother." But he already had. And the contempt in his voice spoke volumes.

I never believed it was because we had talked, but my father always came back. He'd be affectionate and attentive, and my mother would smile again, but then he'd start coming home later and later from work. The steak would burn, my mother would seethe, and it would all blow up again. I felt used and manipulated. I swore many times that I was going to stay out of it. *They could kill each other for all I cared.* But after I learned that my mother *had* actually attempted suicide, I no longer believed I had that option.

"Yes, Ma," I said, "I will speak to my father."

The repetition of their discord exhausted me. Once Howard left to take her home, I collapsed on the sofa.

"Get dressed," Howard said when he got back, "we're going to the party."

I looked at him as if he were crazy. "Get dressed," he said again. "What are you going to do? Sit there and look at the walls?"

I couldn't move.

"Get dressed," he yelled. "I'm not going to sit in the house. It's New Year's Eve. Gail and Lenny are expecting us. Ronny and Florie will be there. Come on. Get up."

I got dressed. We went. I put on a smile. I was a mannequin at a party. Lenny came over and brought me a drink. We spoke for a few minutes, but then he was off, and I was relieved to not have to make conversation. When I finished the drink, I wandered into their den, lay down on the couch, and fell into a stupor. When it was time to leave, no one could rouse me.

"Sprinkle water on her face," someone said.

"How much did she have to drink?" asked another.

"Call an ambulance," someone suggested.

I heard their voices, but I couldn't respond. The distance between them and me felt huge. I was lost in a memory.

I'm four years old and standing in the kitchen doorway, wearing my pajamas with the little red valentine hearts. My mother holds a long knife. She is screaming at my father. She is wearing her old flannel nightgown. Her feet are bare. Her hair is scrambled. Her lips are stretched tight across her teeth. She looks crazy.

"I'll kill you. I'll kill you!" she shrieks at my father.

"What are you doing, Tessie? Put the knife down." He gestures with his hand like a trainer to a puppy. "Down. Tessie, put the knife down."

"Get out or I'll kill you," she hisses, and leaps towards him.

He turns, sees me, hesitates for one second, and then runs out of the house. The door slams.

"You'll be the death of me," she screams after him.

My mother's eyes are wild. She is turning round and round. Suddenly she sees me and stops.

"Go. Lock yourself in the bedroom. Go, or I'll kill you. Go!" she orders. "Don't open the door. Do you hear me? Don't open the door. Don't let me in."

I stare at the knife. I want to run to her and put my arms around her waist, take the knife and put it safely in the drawer, but I am too frightened to move.

She thrusts the knife at me.

"Go!" she screams.

I run to my room. Lock the door and sit on my bed, straight like an arrow. I do not move one inch.

"I'm telling you, call an ambulance," someone said again.

When I managed to open my eyes, Howard was leaning over me, his face red with shame, thinking I was drunk.

"Get up. Let's go," was all he said.

It was December 18, 1970. My mother was calling me several times a day, every day, but this day was an exception. I got one call, in the morning.

"Don't call me today," she said. "I'm going to take a nap."

"That's it, Ma? You're calling to tell me you're taking a nap? Fine, have a good sleep. I won't call you."

I hung up, and though I was puzzled, I resisted the impulse to call her back. She'd been phoning four and five times a day. I'd tried to get Howard to run interference—*tell her I'm not home, out at the supermarket, anything to give me a break*—but instead he'd pick up the phone and say, "She's right here."

As desperate as my mother was to keep her husband, I was desperate to get rid of mine. I would have walked out on Howard in a minute, but with no job, no college, no profession, and no idea how I would raise three kids on my own, I felt stuck.

The night before, I'd lain awake thinking of the many times, as I was growing up, that she'd yell at me that I'd be happy when she was six feet under.

"Admit it, Linda. Don't lie. Admit it," she'd demand.

Terrified that it was true, I'd bury my feelings. But the previous night, I'd decided to take the risk and tell her to stop calling me. *If she kills herself, she kills herself,* I thought. *At least the phone will stop ringing.*

I was getting the kids ready for bed when the phone rang. I braced myself.

"You have to stop," I blurted. "You can't keep calling me all day long. I have three little children. You just can't keep doing this, Ma. Please understand."

"*Understand,* Linda? *You* don't understand. If you understood what he's putting me through, you'd talk to him. He's your father. He'll listen to you."

"Ma, he's a grown man."

"A grown man? Your father, a grown man? Don't make me laugh."

"If he's such an idiot, then why don't you let him go and make your own life?"

"I've told you—he is my life. Do you hear me? Your father *is* my life."

"This is no life, Ma, you're miserable."

"Don't tell me what's a life. Just tell me if he's coming back. That's all I want to know."

My mother didn't know that this time I'd been urging him to stay away. If they couldn't find a life together, then maybe he could find a life alone. I told my mother what I hoped would be the truth.

"No, Ma. I don't think he's coming back. It's been three months."

"It's been almost four months," she corrected.

"Okay, four months. I think you have to face it."

"Face it? What should I face, that I don't have a husband?" she cried. "I should sit back while he runs off with some slut?"

"Ma, you don't know that—"

"What? I don't know that he has somebody? Are you *crazy?*" she yelled. "You always believed your father. It doesn't matter if the proof was right in front of your nose, you believed him. I showed you lipstick on his collar? You still believed him."

"I was fourteen, Ma, and you were telling me that my father was running around. Why would I want to believe that? I was just a kid."

"Well, you're not fourteen anymore."

"Stop! You have to stop," I cried. "You have to let him go."

"Over my dead body," she said.

"All right, then. Over your dead body," I yelled back. "You can't keep doing this."

"Fine," she said. "You want me to stop? I'll stop."

"I'll stop," she repeated, her voice gone cold. "Goodbye, Linda."

Amazingly, the phone didn't ring again until five o'clock that evening.

"How was your nap?" I asked.

"There's five hundred dollars bingo money in the sugar bowl under the sink for you. I won the jackpot," she mumbled.

I knew immediately what she was up to. I panicked. What to do? Keep her talking on the phone and try and get her to help herself, or hang up and call the police?

"Ma. Don't. Please. I'm begging you."

She said nothing.

"Ma? Ma?" I cried into the phone. I could hear her breathing, but she wouldn't speak.

I whispered goodbye, hung up, and called the police.

"My mother's killing herself," I cried. The baby was on my hip. He kept wriggling and trying to grab the phone. I could hear my other two boys playing in their room.

"How do you know she's committing suicide?"

"Because I know, damn it. Believe me. She's tried it before. She's doing it again." My voice was shrill. *These idiots,* I thought. *My mother is dying and they want proof. Her body will be proof if they don't get over there.*

"We can't go into the apartment unless you're there," said the dispatcher.

"What? I have three little kids. I can't—"

"Then we can't."

"All right. All right," I gave in. "It will take me about twenty minutes. I'll meet you there."

I hung up, frantic. What to do with the kids? I couldn't take them with me. I imagined them seeing a hanging Nana, a bleeding Nana, a screaming Nana, or an open window and no Nana. There was no time and no point in calling Howard—he was at work in Manhattan and not due home for another hour. I called my best friend, Susan, who lived nearby. Just as she arrived, the landlady came home. I left the kids with her, and Susan and I rushed to the car. It was cold and raining. Shivering, I realized that I'd forgotten to put on a coat.

My mother must have called her brother Seymour, because when Susan and I arrived at the apartment, a neighbor said that he and the police were already inside. Later, I would learn that there were so many bolts on the door, the police had to enter through the terrace—another twenty minutes wasted.

I banged on the apartment door and Seymour answered, looking like a crazy man.

"Stay out here," he said, and slammed the door.

I was left standing in the hall like a stranger. It was dinnertime. The neighbors, unwilling to let their food get cold, brought their plates with them into the hallway so they could continue eating while they watched real drama instead of the television news. Their faces swam before me, distorted, like images in a funhouse mirror. I closed my eyes to make them disappear.

It took forever for Aunt Dorothy, Seymour's wife to open the door.

"You can come in," she said "but you're *not* to go into the bedroom. I can't let you in the bedroom."

"She's my mother. I want to see her." I began to push through.

"You can't. Please Linda. Just sit . . . please, just sit."

Bewildered, I gave in and sat on the couch. Susan held my hand. I heard activity—muffled voices coming from the bedroom. A policeman came out.

"I'm her daughter," I said. "What's going on?"

"There's a doctor in there with her," was all he said.

All right, I thought. *She's alive. There's a doctor in there with her. We got here in time. She's going to be okay.*

I tried to collect myself while I waited. I looked around the apartment. After twenty-eight years of living in near-empty rooms, my mother finally had an apartment with furniture. She had decorated it like a 1940s movie set with white carpeting, a gold couch, and glass curio cabinets. There were matching, hand-painted vases in each of the cabinets, which my mother had assured me were worth a lot of money.

"They'll be yours someday," she had said. "Along with the ring."

"The ring" was one my father had given her for their twenty-fifth wedding anniversary. It was one of the years he was in the money, and she somehow managed to cajole him into this extravagant purchase—proof positive that he loved her, she told me. I thought it was more a measure of guilt than love. The ring looked like a diamond tiara. I told her it was beautiful, but I knew I would never wear it.

Seymour came out of the bedroom, vomit stains all over his shirt.

"Where's your fucking father?" he screamed. "I'm going to kill him."

From far away, I heard a deep guttural sound.

"Nooooooooo," I moaned.

We sat *shiva* for my mother at Seymour's house. The rabbi gave the immediate family hard wooden benches to sit on. According to Jewish ritual, mourners are not supposed to relax into the comfort of soft chairs. I thought, given the circumstances of my mother's demise, we should have been given a soft chair dispensation, but no one was asking my opinion. My father, a.k.a. "the murderer," was condemned to a far corner of the living room. In a declaration of allegiance, I moved my bench next to his, but that's it, that's all I remember of the *shiva*. I don't know who came to pay their respects or what they said when they got there. For five days, it all swirled around me—I existed in that soundless space between the explosion and the scream.

After the *shiva*, I went back home and tried to resume my normal routine. I dusted the furniture, picked up the kids' toys, and defrosted the chopped meat, but I was haunted. Every Friday evening at five o'clock, the time of her last phone call, I would reimagine her last day, December 18. Getting up. Brushing her teeth. Taking her vitamins. Would she have taken her vitamins? With calm, deliberate motions, I see her pouring a cup of coffee. Sitting down at the dining room table. Lighting a cigarette. The pills, like small vials of colored candy, are lined up in front of her. She opens a bottle and pours them into her hand. I'm horrified, but I'm also aware I don't try to stop her.

She swallowed dozens. Who knows how long she'd been hoarding them?

She'd left suicide notes on little white squares of paper, taped to the kitchen counter.

Mine said: YOU HAVE HOWARD. GRANDMA HAS SAM. I HAVE NO ONE.

My father's note said: I LOVE YOU. BE HAPPY.

The day after she died, friends and relatives rushed to her apartment and picked their notes off the counter, like place cards at a bar mitzvah.

I did not cry at my mother's funeral. I convinced myself that someone else was in the coffin, a distant relative, a peripheral acquaintance, someone who had been very sick for a long time, and wasn't it a relief that she was finally out of her misery? I sat in the pew, looked up at the stained-glass window, and thought of nothing. No tears. No expression. Numb like a corpse. *You have a cold heart*, said a familiar voice inside my head.

My mother-in-law came over to me in the vestibule of the funeral home.

"Linda, don't worry," she said in a conspiratorial whisper, "I've told everyone that your mother had a heart attack."

"Well, then you're going to look like a liar," I said, "because I intend to tell everyone the truth."

She looked at me as if I were crazy. I didn't care. I'd had it with secrets.

My mother had fiercely warned me from as far back as I could remember, that whatever went on inside the house was to stay inside the house. I was to pretend we had a happy home. I went through childhood terrified, never quite sure what I should or shouldn't say.

Well now the word was out, and *she'd* given the family's secrets away, not me. I was finally free to speak the truth to anyone who asked. If they didn't ask, I found a way to slip it into the conversation.

"Oh, how old is Eric now? Really? Four already? Geez, time goes fast. Did you know that my mother killed herself?"

Or "Sally, I saw Norman the other day; did he tell you that my mother killed herself?"

I was particularly excited to run into someone I didn't know so I could tell it fresh.

"So nice to meet you. You may have heard that my mother killed herself."

"Oh, my God," they would mutter. "I'm so sorry. How awful for you."

The brazen would ask for details: "I hope you don't mind my asking, but how did she do it?"

"Pills," I'd answer.

"What a shock! Who found her? Did you find her?"

I didn't mind them asking. The more they wanted to know, the more I could go over it. I didn't have to embellish the story, because it was gruesome in its own right. Their shock reflected my own. There was something in the telling and retelling that helped make it real.

A month after the funeral, Howard and I went to the movies to see *I Never Sang for My Father*, the story of a man whose mother dies, leaving him to care for a father he hated. The film opened with black letters on a white screen that read, DEATH ENDS A LIFE. BUT IT DOES NOT END A RELATIONSHIP, WHICH STRUGGLES ON IN THE SURVIVOR'S MIND, TOWARD SOME RESOLUTION, WHICH IT MAY NEVER FIND.

Oh my God, I thought, *I'm condemned. It will never be over. She will haunt me till the day I die. I will never find peace.*

The movie ended, the dam broke, and I began to sob. I couldn't get out of my seat. Howard was embarrassed.

"Shush," he said. "People are looking at you like you're crazy."

"*Crazy?* I'm not crazy. My mother was crazy. I'm not my mother," I sobbed. "I am not my mother," I pleaded.

"Let's just go," he said.

On December 18, 1971, at five o'clock—one year to the hour of her last phone call—I went to the kitchen, and stood before the *yahrzeit* memorial candle. The kids were with Howard. I had the house to myself. I recited the mourners' Kaddish: "*Yit'gadal v'yitkadash sh'mei raba.*" I didn't understand the words, but I understood that if the purpose of the Kaddish was to honor her life and ease her way out of purgatory into heaven then I took issue with the Jewish law that denies mourning rites for suicides. I imagined the vast beyond to be impossible to navigate, even given a proper death. I lit the candle, finished the prayer, and began to talk to her as if she could hear me. I wanted her to know that by changing my life, I'd hoped to give meaning to her death.

"I've been busy since you left. It's only been a year, but I've moved to New Jersey, started college, and separated from Howard. The kids and I are on our own now, Ma, and it's good. It's good to be free."

What I didn't say was how stupid I thought it was to kill herself over a man, and how angry I was that she left me.

I moved the candle to the corner of the counter, and shut the light. These candles were ensconced in thick glass, protecting the flame from going out during the twenty-four hours of remembrance.

Around two in the morning, I awoke, flooded with memories of our last phone call. Once again, I questioned my decision to get off the line and call the police. *What if I'd stayed on the phone? Could I have talked her out of it? How many pills had she taken before she called? Was it enough to kill her? Did she know at that time that the deed was done?*

I felt an urgent need to go downstairs and look at the candle. The house was cold. I was naked. When I got to the kitchen, I was relieved to see the candle still burning, but as I stood there, staring, it flickered and died.

There was no draft in the room. No open window. No explanation.

Just another way to say goodbye.

⌒ feng shui in the *shtetl* ⌒

Feng (wind) shui (water) is a Chinese system that uses the laws of heaven and earth to help one improve life in order to achieve harmony and positive qi, energy. You probably know that there is good qi and bad qi. Of course, everybody wants to have good qi. Bad qi is toxic, like a bad smell. Nobody wants to be around people with bad qi. You use feng shui to arrange your spaces so that you and your house will give off good qi. Here are a few feng shui rules: declutter your house, make sure you have good quality air and light, find out your birth element and decorate accordingly—if it is fire, make sure your fabrics are orange and yellow. Also, find out your lucky direction. For example, Jews know they have to face east when praying except when they are in Israel and get to pray at the Western Wall. For Muslims, it's more complicated; from what I can understand the direction of prayer, *Qibla*, has changed over the years and created some confusion. I'm not Muslim, so I don't know how to solve their feng shui problem. As for Christians, as far as I can see, their lucky direction is always up. Also, you should be sure that your house and your grave face in your lucky direction. I've no idea how to find your lucky direction or why qi even matters after you're dead.

Feng shui was very popular in the suburbs in the '70s. When women weren't going to consciousness-raising groups where they discussed the pros and cons of walking around naked in front of their children or to masturbation workshops where they were comparing paintings by Georgia O'Keefe to photos of female genitalia, they were feng shuing their houses and getting rid of clutter. This process usually began by getting a divorce, which is still the best way I know to clean out closets. In the '70s, in the suburbs, husbands were being tossed out like old shoes. On my block alone, seven husbands hit the curb, and as many closets were reclaimed.

My house was in a New Jersey bedroom community. (I ask you, what exactly *is* a bedroom community?) We were following the qi,energy, out of Brooklyn to the burbs. If we had known it was going to turn around and go back again, we might have just hung out and waited, because I can tell you that there was no good qi in New Jersey. We bought a split-level house on a road with more split-level houses, a faded gray with black shutters. It had a big backyard where the kids were supposed to want to play. It had a thorny, wild rose hedge that separated our backyard from our neighbors. This was definitely a feng shui hedge for us, because all the debris that blew down from the 7-Eleven store on the corner stopped on their side of the hedge. The neighbors wanted us to take the hedge down. We said, "What, are you kidding?" That was the end of good neighborly qi. I suppose they got some secret delight watching the crabapples drop off the big crabapple tree in our front yard, where they soon went soft and wormy. I didn't want to pick them up and neither did my kids, so they rotted in the heat, wafting a bad odor through the kitchen window. Bad qi.

My husband Howard, having found another bedroom community, left me with the three kids and the house—the

Kramer v. Kramer joint custody thing hadn't caught on yet, so I was happily on my own and in full charge of our progeny. After he left, I looked around the house with a fresh feng shui eye. The small den-TV room had lime-green shag carpeting left by the former owner, with one white, ink-marked, swivel leather chair and one large, blue, beanbag chair. The white walls had recently been decorated by my three-year-old.

The living room wasn't much better. It had gray carpeting, a mosaic-tiled coffee table missing some of its chips, and a red velvet, flocked couch with plastic seat covers. The couch was a hand-me-down from my mother, who made me promise I would not remove the seat covers. I explained that in winter the couch was cold, and in summer it made an embarrassing sucking sound when you got up. My mother was dead, but she still could play on my guilt. I could hear the conversation in my head.

Your uncle Seymour is in the plastic slipcover business. What's he going to think when he comes out to Jersey to see you?

"Uncle Seymour has never stepped foot out of Brooklyn."

He'd come if you invited him. Two years you are in the house and you never had a housewarming. Now it's too late. How warm is a house without a husband?

And then to rub it in: *Grandma's worried about you: she doesn't know who's going to want a woman with three children.*

"Why do I need a husband?" I said as much to myself as to her, pointing to my T-shirt that said A WOMAN WITHOUT A MAN IS LIKE A FISH WITHOUT A BICYCLE.

My grandmother, who had spent her married life taking care of five children and a husband who wouldn't lift a finger, and my mother, who had spent hers holding on to a husband who never held on to her, still could not imagine the joy of being alone. I promised myself that as soon as the house had good qi, I'd invite the family. She'd have had no idea what I was talking about.

That's just an excuse.

I couldn't argue. She was right. Our best conversations ended when I stopped trying to wrestle the alligator.

With the implicit support of Betty Friedan and Gloria Steinem, I asserted my new will and took the plastic off the couch. I would have gotten rid of the coffee table, but I needed something to put a cup of coffee on and a place to put my feet up. I tried to color in the missing chips with crayons. It didn't work, but you had to appreciate my resourcefulness and effort. Being separated gave me energy.

I believe that some people have an innate feng shui sensibility. If you knew what came first and where to put it, you didn't have to hire a feng shui expert. In the '70s everybody who thought they were somebody was hiring these experts. I don't know where they found them. Maybe there was a feng shui directory. All I know was that I wasn't buying. My qi fluctuated with my mood, and my mood seemed to fluctuate with who knows what—but my feng shui was solid. Here's the evidence: I knew that a core feng shui principle comes with a less-is-more philosophy. It fits with the decluttering factor. I intuitively knew this, which is why I was able to convince my husband to spend *more* money on *less* furniture. We invested all of our wedding money on three knock-out pieces: a Danish teakwood dining table and six curved-back matching chairs with black leather seats; a hand-painted, green-lacquered, Chinese commode that was out-of-sight gorgeous and had natural China qi; and a large, cherry wood, crescent-shaped desk, with an inlaid leather top.

When we split, my husband, in his desire to make an imposing statement by leaving a large space, took the desk. That was fine with me. I moved the Chinese commode into the vacancy he left. I oiled the teakwood table, and that was it for the furniture. I went to the lumberyard and picked up pine planks, a saw, and a hammer. I made my own bookcases, because in my quest to find my own lucky direction, I had started college and needed a place to put my books. I stained the shelves Jacobean brown. The kids and I distressed them with hammers. I placed the planks on bricks, stacked the books in alphabetical order, looked around, and felt instant, strong and ego-filled qi. Lastly, I went into the bedroom, pulled the curtains off the windows, and let the room fill with air and light.

My friend Elsa was taking a course with one of those feng shui experts and was deeply immersed in chakras and baguas. She insisted that I hadn't done enough, and that there would be no harmony in my house without the proper application of all the feng shui principles. I told her that the harmony had arrived when my husband left.

"Yes, but what about your inner turmoil? What about the space within?" I told her that I was working on my inner turmoil in therapy. I was sifting through my unconscious, sorting through my history, looking desperately for any evidence of ancestral harmony. I was currently focused on the *shtetl*.

According to my grandmother, hers was a small house outside of Berditchever. It had two rooms, a dirt floor, six kids, and a sewing machine. My grandmother, the oldest daughter, worked the sewing machine. She cut off and mangled the tip of her pointer finger making white shirts for the Cossacks. They liked the shirts but raided the *shtetl* anyway. I'm sure there was no feng shui in the *shtetl*. When you are running from the Cossacks, you're not worried about how the furniture is arranged. Grandma escaped to the forest where she lived until she got a ticket for the boat. America was her lucky direction. Grandma was in steerage. By the third day, everybody was seasick, and whatever good qi had come on board had been thrown up and out the portholes. I think the good qi came back when they stood on deck and saw the Statue of Liberty. Grandma said she was so happy, she cried. When I was a kid, I'd make her tell this story over and over, particularly the parts about the Statue of Liberty and her mangled finger. There is harmony in stories of survival.

Let's face it, all the immigrants coming to America were looking for better qi. Grandma hoped to find it when she climbed the four flights to her aunt Rifka's apartment on Avenue A. Instead she found three rooms, eight people and one bathroom down the hall. Each night the furniture was re-arranged, not for feng shui, but for sleeping. The kitchen became a bedroom. Grandma was fourteen years old. They figured she still had a good back, so she slept on a board that was laid across two sawhorses. If she hadn't been the last relative to arrive, she might have gotten the table, but her uncle who worked all day as a presser in a shop got the table. Grandma didn't speak English, but she knew how to sew. She landed a job at the Triangle Shirtwaist Factory. I can tell you that there was definitely no feng shui at that factory.

Grandma told me she only worked at the Triangle for one month. She said that when her mother, back in Russia, found out that her daughter had to work on *Shabbes*, the Sabbath, she asked the rabbi in the *shtetl* to write a letter to America and tell her daughter that there is no harmony in Hell. Grandma listened to her mother and quit the factory. Two weeks later, the factory burned down. Grandma said that the moral of the story is to always observe *Shabbes*. My mother said that the moral of the story was to always listen to your mother.

After a couple of years, Rifka and her daughters decided a plank in the kitchen added nothing to the décor, and to de-clutter the apartment, someone had to go. They decided that it was fitting that the last one in should be the first one out. Everyone but Grandma agreed, and they chipped in and hired a matchmaker to find a husband for Grandma. They must have hired the cheapest matchmaker they could find, because she picked Harry.

Harry was no bargain. They married and moved to Brooklyn. They had five children—Hymie, Izzy, Tessie (my mother), Seymour, and Ethel—and an apartment at the back. Apartments at the back have no chance of feng shui. They face walls and alleys. They have no light, no air. They come with envy for everyone who lives in the front. Envy is bad qi.

Grandma said that when her children were young, her apartment was like little boxes, tiny rooms with rails on the windows. The windows looked out on brick walls. The apartment was on the sixth floor of a walkup. If you have ever carried groceries for five children and a husband up six floors, you know that there was no good qi in that apartment. But Grandma had an eye for color, and she knew how to sew. At Passover, flowered, linen slipcovers appeared on the furniture. The rug with pockmarks from Harry's cigarette ashes was rolled up and the wood floors polished. The rose-colored dishes we ate off all year were exchanged for the pure white plates that had sat in the back of the cupboard through the winter. When all was done, Grandma would take a minute, sit down, and look at all her hard work with a big, happy, feng shui smile.

For the first five years of my life, I spent most of my time at Grandma's. Trust me when I tell you this was a good thing. My parents were too busy and too angry to deal with a little kid. There was bad qi and no harmony in my house. Staying at Grandma's was fine with me. By the time I was born, all but one of Grandma's children had been launched and were out trying to find their own lucky directions, except Aunt Ethel who had left and was back again.

When I was a kid, my mother said I was a "little *pisher* with big ears." That meant to bug off and stop listening to grownup conversation. But I liked grownup conversation, particularly when they whispered or spoke in Yiddish. I had to be a *pisher* with big ears because no one would tell me anything except that I was too young to know about "such things." I knew enough to know that I wanted to know more. Sometimes I'd pick up a little, listening to the yelling at the weekly poker game. If I got out of bed and peeked in from the bedroom, I'd see them sitting around the table: a cigarette dangling from

Grandpa Harry's lips, handsome Malconson smiling up at Grandma, and Sam Kushner reluctant as always to ante up. Mrs. Malconson, the Webers, and Gussie Kushner just kept their heads down and played their cards. They'd been friends forever. They had all come over from the same part of Russia, and they were all members of the Berditchever cemetery club.

I don't know what to tell you about the poker game except that everybody's luck seemed to go in cross directions. It wasn't about winning, but more about who passed which card, and why that card and not the other card, and why they pulled for an inside straight when they didn't stand a chance and kept the person who should have gotten the card from getting the full house they deserved. They argued in Yiddish. They argued in English. It didn't matter. I got it, that you can have love without harmony, that good qi and bad qi can go together, and that a lot depended on the cards you were dealt. I can tell you, though, that if you wanted pure, uncorrupted, unconflicted harmony and good qi, you had to have been there when Grandma and I were alone.

We had our routine. The day started with me sitting on the toilet with the lid down, helping Grandma dress. It was there that I first learned that there was feng shui dressing, and that clothes, properly arranged, could be art. It was my job to hand Grandma each garment in exactly the right order. It began with a salmon-colored undershirt and cotton bloomers to match. The undershirt, she told me, was to keep the corset and the bra from getting smelly. Next, I handed her the corset. The corset was my favorite. It had bones and crisscrossed laces that wrapped on hooks from the bottom to the top. It was like cats-in-the-cradle, a game with fingers and string that Grandma played in the *shtetl*. Grandma told me that if I wanted to be straight as an arrow, I should always wear a corset and sit on a hard chair. By the time I hit adolescence, the corset had been replaced by the girdle, equally restrictive, and also guaranteed to keep you from ever taking a deep breath. After

Grandma laced the corset, she put on the bra, and after the bra, the slip. Finally, at the end, came the dress. After that, we left the house and said hello to the yentas sitting on the stoop. We went to see Sam at the vegetable stand, to get the greens for the soup, and to Herbie the butcher for a nice brisket.

The butcher shop had sawdust on the floor, a finger on the scale, and Esther, the chicken plucker, in the corner. Esther wore a black dress and a bloodstained apron. She sat, legs spread, on a wooden stool with a dead chicken on her lap. If you replicated Sam's stand and Herbie's shop for, say, a movie set or a play, it would have a historical feng shui—a perfect reflection of life in Brooklyn in the 1940s.

I did not come of age in the sixties—if you ask me, that was the feng shui generation. I missed that boat by just a few years, and forever after I was out of my element. When I was in high school in Brooklyn, girls were getting pinned when they were sophomores and engagement rings by graduation. I managed to hold off and not walk down the aisle till I was nineteen, but I still missed the whole getting high, Janis Joplin, free love thing. I can tell you right now that had I not been a they-won't-respect-you-in-the-morning good girl—had I had sex before I got married, there would have been no divorce because there would have been no marriage. There was no harmony or good qi in sex with Howard.

When the festival was happening, I wanted to strap my baby on my back and head up to Woodstock. Howard said I was crazy. I argued that all the good qi was on the New York State Thruway, heading in what should have been *our* lucky direction. He turned on the television and showed me how it was raining, and how they were all stuck in traffic. Nothing was moving. I watched the news all day. I told him they looked like they were moving and shaking to me, sliding in the mud, happy as clams. He said, "Yeah. That's because they are high on weed and LSD." I said, "Yeah, so?"

In my fantasy, had I gone directly to college, there still might have been time for me to crash that party, but there was no money for tuition, and we had to move again—not because we couldn't find our lucky direction but because my father couldn't find a way to pay the rent. The only thing that was permanent was the storage unit—the receptacle for all the clutter we accumulated from one move to another that wouldn't fit into wherever it was that we were moving to this time. So here it was: the year I was graduating from high school, and, once again, we were up and out. We moved into Grandma's apartment, which marked the end of Grandma's harmony. All her kids were out of the house, even Ethel, and Grandpa Harry was dead. Grandma celebrated her newfound freedom by getting herself an apartment in the front. She had air. She had light. She had a view of the street where she could sit and sew by the window. And now, in *mitn derinnen*, in the middle of everything, she had us. It was like she was back at Rifka's.

Meanwhile, my father, believing the only thing worse than being broke was *looking* broke, went out and bought a new Chrysler New Yorker convertible. When we saw him drive up to the house with the top down and a big grin, Grandma went into the kitchen and hacked a chicken, my mother went nuts and started to scream, and I, realizing that my father had no representation, stood up on a pulpit and, with a combination of insight and audacity, preached the importance of the welfare Cadillac. My mother said, "Fine, then you get yourself a job and make the car payments, because he doesn't have two cents." My father for once applauded my mother. I joined Grandma and the chicken in the kitchen. My father turned the car around and drove off in his new lucky direction.

Where feng shui used heaven and earth to help improve life, my father relied on money and charm; the charm was his, the money generally wasn't. The money belonged to the business, his partner, the bank, or the mafia. Like a shell game, he moved it around from one to the other, as dictated by the

necessity of the moment and his desire to stay out of jail—
or worse yet, a ditch. His personal element must have been
water, given the way money ran through his fingers. Picture
my father, and you'll see he's wearing a well-tailored suit and a
white shirt with French cuffs. He wears the star sapphire ring
on his right hand, and no wedding band on his left. He looks
taller than he is. Some women said he was Errol Flynn, others
said he was Clark Gable without the ears. My mother said he
was an empty promise.

The pictures of my mother from the late '30s and early
'40s, before she married my father, show that she had a defi-
nite feng shui style and some pretty sexy qi. She had Swedish
features: blonde hair, perky nose, and pale white skin. In one
picture, she is wearing Kate Hepburn trousers, a jacket fitted
at the waist with shoulder pads, and a blouse with a jabot. In
just a head shot, the kind you got from a booth with a curtain,
she is wearing my father's Stetson hat tipped to the side. My
father's chin is resting on her shoulder. He is looking at the
camera; she is looking at him. My mother will brag and tell you
that people said she looked like Tina Louise, the sexy actress
with sultry lips. I did not know this version of my mother. The
mother I knew wore a beehive hairdo and butterfly glasses.
Her feng shui must have gone into storage during one of my
father's *situations.*

I shouldn't point a finger at my mother, because I was
certainly not a feng shui kid, which caused my mother a lot
of anxious qi. There's a picture of me at eleven: long, skinny
legs like a pony and a Buster Brown haircut with bangs cut too
short. I have scabs and bruises from popping wheelies on my
bicycle. I'm an ace at dodgeball, and the only girl allowed on
the boys' baseball team. My mother had a very clear picture
of what a daughter should be like, and I wasn't it. In an effort
to edge me towards a more feminine feng shui, she taught
me how to rumba. That wasn't enough, so my mother began
to make mother-daughter outfits the way my grandma made

slipcovers. I particularly remember the yellow calico dresses with the puritan collars, edged in red rickrack. We tried them on and stood in front of the mirror. Think Diane Arbus, and you'll get the picture. To have some harmony, I agreed to wear it, but only if I could cut school and we could go to the movies. I figured it was dark at the movie. We put on our dresses and went to see *The Moon is Blue*—a racy, no kids allowed, 1953 romantic comedy about two men, William Holden and David Niven, who go after a woman, Maggie McNamara, who is determined to keep her virginity. I leaned over and whispered to my mother that if Maggie wore one of these dresses she'd have had nothing to worry about. This was the beginning of bad adolescent qi.

After we moved in and my father bought the car, there was no harmony left in Grandma's house. Grandma kept feeding Candy the collie Jewish food—kreplach and flanken. Her colitis was getting worse, and I was tired of cleaning up after her. If I was going to make the car payments, I needed to get a job. My father, knowing the garment center, told me my lucky direction was 1407 Broadway. He said to knock on the door of every showroom until someone said "yes." He told me, so I wouldn't be scared, to picture the guys who interviewed me as sitting on the toilet. Aside from *Don't listen to your mother*, it was the only good advice he ever gave me. Correction: he also advised me not to marry Howard. He was right on all three accounts.

The guy sitting on the toilet turned out to be my new boss at Century of Boston. He really was an ass. He had the pompous attitude of many short men, who tried to make up in arrogance what they lacked in height. He thought he was passing for tall because he stood on his father's shoulders. His name was Alan, insisting that the emphasis be on the second syllable. If it weren't for Oscar, Alan's father, Alan would have just been another little *pisher*. He strutted around the office sucking air through his teeth, obsessively checking the Teletype machine like a newspaper reporter expecting big news. Oscar knew that Alan was an ass, but he had to do something with his youngest son, so he stuck him in the New York showroom. There was no good qi between Oscar and Alan. It was so bad that when Oscar was in town, there was no harmony in the showroom at all. Alan hid in our office till Oscar left, bossing us around like a tyrant.

It turned out that Howard was a tyrant too. It didn't take long after our feng shui wedding to realize that this was going to be a very bad marriage, but, following Grandma's lead, I tried to hang in there. After twelve miserable years, I accepted that Grandma's mistake didn't have to be mine, and that no matter how much you pray, there can be no feng shui if there is no harmony.

I learned feng shui wasn't just about wind and water, but about comfort with order, like the steps and stages of my grandmother putting on her garments—one thing leads to another. Bad marriages can end, unlucky directions can be reversed, and harmony with oneself precedes harmony with another.

sharks and other perils

This was my day, not every day, but often enough. I'd get up in the morning, get my three kids ready and off to school, do my homework until 3:00, and if I was lucky enough not to have to go food shopping or do other intrusive errands, pick them up at school, pile into my old Oldsmobile 88, rush directly into the City for auditions, run around town to various ad agencies where most of the time they had to say inane things like, "If it isn't Heinz, it isn't ketchup," drive home and hope to beat the rush hour traffic, feed them dinner, say hello to the babysitter and goodbye to the kids, with a reminder that bedtime was 9:00, *and I'm not kidding*, then head to school for a 7:30 class. At 11:00 I was settled in bed and at 11:01 I was asleep.

This marathon began in 1974, about a year and a half after Howard and I split, when he phoned with an unusual invitation. He had shown a picture of our boys, aged four, seven, and nine, to a business associate who was dating Delores Reed, a talent manager.

"Delores was excited when she saw the picture," he said.

"Why?" I asked.

"Because they're cute."

"Lots of kids are cute."

"Yeah, but not all kids have red hair. Red hair is the draw. Redheaded kids look good on color TV," he said. "She's just starting her talent management business. We'd be getting in on the ground floor."

"What do you mean, *we*? Unless you're planning to take off work and run around Manhattan to auditions, there's no *we* here."

"What are you starting, Linda? Every time I talk to you, it's a fight. I'm encouraging you to do this. It could be good money."

"Well it wouldn't be your money—or my money, for that matter; it would be the kids' money."

He was right. I was angry. I figured he was having dreams of reducing his child support from a pittance to a penny, but, before we hung up, I agreed to consider it.

We were poor. The kids were on the free lunch program at school. The money situation was tough, but I was happier than I had been for the twelve years Howard and I had been together. When we moved to East Brunswick, New Jersey, I started at Rutgers University, and, when Howard announced that he'd met a lovely young girl and was leaving the marriage, I said "Thank you, God," and asked if I could help him pack.

Now Howard was presenting me with a moral dilemma. I didn't want to exploit my kids, but I also wanted to send them to summer camp and put money away for their future. Howard was pushing me to get a job, as if taking care of three little kids on my own was a paid vacation. I had no skills, and minimum wage jobs did not pay for childcare, and now that I had gotten myself to college, I was determined to stay in school.

Every other weekend when Howard came to pick up the kids, he brought up Delores.

"She wants to know what you've decided."

I'd been dating George for about a year. He was tall with

gray hair and a gray mustache and beautiful hands. He looked like Omar Sharif and I immediately thought of my great movie escape to see *Dr. Zhivago* perhaps because I was madly in love and eager to please his opinion carried a lot of weight. When we met, he was playing Milos Glorioso in a community theatre production of *A Funny Thing Happened on the Way to the Forum*, where he got to strut around the stage and make loud proclamations. I couldn't tell if it was the acting he loved or the throng of New Jersey housewives, dressed in skimpy Grecian garb, fawning all over him. He was strongly encouraging me to go with it. George had a presence and a paternal authority—he shared my father's name and also spoke with the confidence of someone who "knows." Nevertheless, I was resistant to trust the opinion of a frustrated thespian. I would go round and round in my head.

What effect would this have on the kids? Would they still be able to have normal childhoods, or would the auditions and the shoots become all-consuming? What would happen to their little egos? If they were successful, would they become stars instead of kids? And how would they feel if they have no success—all the time and energy put into the project with no payoff? What would happen to their egos then? And what about me? Would I turn into one of those stage mothers drawn to the glamour? I'd always been a movie nut— wouldn't it be amazing to have your kids in film? Yes, but you know what happens to kid stars, most of them end up on the analyst's couch. Well, that could happen anyway. At least they'd have the money to pay for it.

I tortured myself for a month, and then I finally said yes.

I sat the kids down and tried to explain what it was we were about to do. David, my nine-year-old, got excited. He'd been star struck since he was three, and he saw this as his chance to make it big. Jonathan, my seven-year-old, not liking his current teacher, asked hopefully if he'd get to miss school, and Robbie, only four, took his cue from his older brother and jumped up and down with feigned excitement.

"Don't get too excited," I said. "I don't know if this is going to work, but here are the rules of the game—everything is going to be shared. I don't know which of you will have success, but given that you're all going to be inconvenienced, it seems only fair that the earnings be equally divided. And, if you have an important play date, soccer game, or for that matter, anything else you really want to do, we will forgo the audition. And," I went on, "I promise that your mother will not turn into a pushy stage mother."

When we went up for auditions, I could always spot the stage mothers. They would sit, waiting their next, primping and preening their kid, going over and over the script, gossiping about who got what part for which commercial. They would talk about the idiocy of the casting director for not casting Suzie or Ethan or whomever their little horse-in-the-race happened to be. They sucked up to the mothers whose kids were cast most often, comparing agents and talent managers. I sat there reading Freud's *Psychopathology of Everyday Life* for my psychology class, trying not to engage in conversation. I got a reputation for being aloof, but I didn't care. I didn't want to get caught up in the fervor and, to my credit, I did try to hold the line. This was not easy, as every time Delores Reed called, she would dangle fame and fortune and beg me to bring them into the city.

"It's a callback," she'd say.

"I'm sorry, but we can't come in."

"Come on, Linda, it's Fruit Loops. It could end up being three commercials. It could end up being a whole campaign. You don't turn down a callback." I would start to hear panic in her voice. "You'll get day rates, and then every time it shows, you'll get residuals. You're looking at big bucks, and you know that cereals run. Every show for kids has a cereal spot."

Callbacks were certainly better than no-backs, but there was still no guarantee. All it usually meant was that they had narrowed the field from thirty kids to ten. Everything seemed to hinge on the whim of the director, his need to please the account, and his *vision* for the spot. It was great that my children were getting callbacks, but it was far from a guarantee that they would get the commercial.

Delores collected 10 percent on every gig the kids got. My telling her that I was sorry but Jonathan had been invited to his friend Rodney Yap's birthday party affected her bottom line.

"It's a big deal invitation," I explained. "Only three kids got invited. His mother cooks authentic Chinese food, and, besides, Jonathan's already been to the city this week."

"Jonathan cares that there's Chinese food? You're kidding me. He's seven years old and he's a gourmet? And what's with this Rodney—he only has three friends?"

"Jonathan *loves* Mrs. Yap's cooking," I embellished. "I'm not going to tell him that he can't go to his best friend's birthday party, and that's that."

"This is no way to run a business," she said.

"My children aren't a *business*," I countered. "They are kids who happen to have red hair, and a single mother who's broke, going to college herself, and needing to find a way to save up so that when the time comes she can send *them* to college, because there is no way their father is ever going to do it. You may forget, but I won't, that they are children first and actors second, and I will not compromise their childhood for this *business*, as you call it!"

Delores would back off. I would hang up and then the doubts would rise up and threaten my resolve. *What is the point of doing this whole business if I'm going to do it half-assed? And Delores is right, Fruit Loops are a big deal and Jonathan wants to go to Rodney's birthday party today, but he may not even care tomorrow, and, for all I know, Mrs. Yap is doing takeout.*

I struggled most when Delores called with movie auditions.

"I have an audition tomorrow for Rob," Delores said. "It's big. Spielberg is directing it."

"What is it?"

"It's called *Jaws*."

"Is it a monster movie? I don't want my kids in monster movies."

"It's not a monster movie. It's about a shark. All I can tell you it that it's a big deal movie. It's got a big budget and they are looking to cast a bunch of kids. He's an extra so it's day rates, but you never know, with a kid as cute as Robbie, he could get upgraded to a principal in a minute, and then you are looking at big bucks."

I didn't say anything.

"Are you going to give me a hard time?" she asked.

"I'm thinking."

"What's to *think*? It's a major motion picture. These opportunities don't come along every day." She sighed. "Linda, if you don't want the call, I've got another kid who will take it in a minute."

"Let me ask you one question—does he get eaten?"

"What do you mean, *does he get eaten?*"

"I mean does he get eaten by the shark? I don't want my kid eaten, and I don't want him to be in a movie that would be too frightening to take him to see. Would you take your kid to a movie where he's going to see himself get eaten?"

"I don't know if he gets eaten," she said.

"Find out and call me back."

Fifteen minutes later the phone rang.

"He gets eaten," she whispered.

"What?"

"He gets eaten," she said again.

"Then forget it." I hung up.

While David was the most excited and hopeful of the three kids, it soon became apparent that Jonathan, who couldn't have cared less, was getting most of the calls. David, to compensate for his disappointment and frustration with me for my less-than-wholehearted devotion to the *family biz*, as he liked to call it, apprenticed himself to Delores. They would talk, and, when I was reluctant to go into the city yet again, he'd argue her case. He was good at it and often convinced me to schlep in, particularly and understandably, if the call was for him.

Jonathan provided the entertainment for the trips back and forth to the city. He had made up a cast of characters—each had their own accent, personality, and story to tell. There was Lazy Luba, the ninety-year-old tennis instructor; Timmy the trash can; and Buzzy the bee, who taught brail to blind bumblebees. We'd be sitting in traffic, and, to relieve the tension, one of us would ask Jon to check in on Lazy or Buzzy and see what they were up to. Jon would spin a yarn, but leave the conclusion for the next trip into the city. And when we went up for auditions, we were never quite sure what he was going to pull. For example, once we were on our way up to an audition at a prominent ad agency. There was a very fat man behind us in the elevator. When the elevator door opened, Jonathan turned around, put his arms around the man, kissed him on the belly, looked up at his face, and, deadpan, said, "I think I'll call you Seymour," turned around, and walked out of the elevator.

Jonathan got the part of Spanky in the Our Gang promotion for Marx Toys. This was a big break. It was a series of commercials with the same cast of kids. The money started to roll in, and I was able to send the three kids to summer camp, attend all three summer sessions at school, and make up the twelve credits I'd been unable to take during fall and spring semesters.

We had been in the *biz* for two years when Jonathan got a call to audition to play little Alvy Singer in *Annie Hall*. We'd been calling him "little Woody Allen" since he was a baby.

When he was born with ABO blood incompatibility and had to have all of his blood replaced one cc at a time with O positive donor blood, we often wondered if it was this traumatic beginning that made him such a funny, irreverent, and neurotic kid or if they'd simply given him Woody Allen's blood. Add to that the red hair and horn-rimmed glasses, and there was no doubt that Jon would get the part.

The first day on the *Annie Hall* set, he walked behind Allen, mimicking his gait and gestures. He was so good at it that some of the crew thought he was Allen's son. Had they talked to Jonathan, they would have been further convinced, because Jonathan, like Allen, was by nature a fatalist and a hypochondriac. He was nine years old, but already convinced he had Alzheimer's because he couldn't remember the name of the head of the PLO. So when they shot the first scene in the movie where little Alvy Singer is sitting in the doctor's office and asking what the point is in doing his homework because the universe is expanding, no script was necessary. Jonathan could easily have improvised the scene.

Jonathan at nine was a working actor. He was on the set every day. I was going crazy trying to balance the shoot, the three kids, and studying for finals. I wished I could have gone to the shoot every day, but there was no way I could manage it. It was no trouble finding friends and family to take him in, as everybody wanted the opportunity to be on the set, but no one more than I. David was dying to go in—one day I allowed him to cut school so he could go and watch. It was exciting, but also hard for him to see his brother so laissez-faire when he would have turned cartwheels for the opportunity to be in the film. Robbie didn't seem to mind as long as I got him to his soccer games. He had just made goalie, and, as far as he was concerned, he already was a star.

It didn't take long for Woody Allen to realize that he'd cast a gem in Jonathan. He began writing new scenes for him, some of which ended up in the movie and some on the cutting room floor.

There was the Coney Island bumper car ride: Jonathan was strapped into his car and Woody Allen, infamous for not directing his actors, just told Jonathan to have fun. Jonathan had never been on the bumper car ride, but he was a natural for the scene. The buzzer went off, and he went nowhere. He frantically turned the wheel but he couldn't get any traction. He just sat there getting bumped from all sides. They shot the scene in one take and it was included in the film.

The Brooke Shields scene took a lot longer and ended up on the cutting room floor. Few people know that Brooke was ever in *Annie Hall*, but Jonathan would never forget—he couldn't take his eyes off her.

The scene was set up in an old Brooklyn schoolhouse with chipped plaster walls and a funky smell. A Thanksgiving play was arranged on the wooden stage. Children, dressed as Pilgrims, milled around a town square. Little Alvy Singer, head pushed forward and arms dangling, was in the stockade. In sight was a beautiful young girl in a white dress—Brooke Shields. Jonathan was entranced. There was no acting necessary. Later, on the ride home he told me that she was the most beautiful girl he had ever seen and that he was in love.

The scene took forever to set—getting the lighting just right, angling the cameras, instructing each child as to their position on the stage and their role in the play. Jonathan, stuck in the stockade, didn't mind the wait. His eyes followed Brooke around the room.

Brooke was on the set with her mother, Teri, who it was later said, "controlled her career with an iron fist." Teri and I sat together and watched the shoot. When she heard I was studying psychology, she wanted my opinion on the part that Brooke was up for in a Louis Malle movie, *Pretty Baby*.

"She plays the role of a young prostitute in a bordello. She has a nude scene. Everybody is making such a fuss. Like, I shouldn't be letting my kid play a part like this, but she's not going to grow up to be a prostitute, so I don't know what they're yakking about. You see my point. You agree, right?" Teri asked.

I didn't know what to say. She was asking the wrong person. I wouldn't let my kid get eaten by a mechanical shark, so I certainly wouldn't have let him get naked.

"It's a tough spot to be in," I said.

"Not really," she answered. "It isn't tough for me. It's a Louis Malle movie. Louis Malle is a very respected French film director. You don't turn down a Louis Malle movie."

She was sounding more and more like Delores.

"Would you mind giving us a ride to Penn Station?" Teri asked, "I didn't bring my car."

"Happy to do it," I lied, knowing that going from Brooklyn to Manhattan and then out to Jersey was going to get us stuck in traffic. However, I figured if they ended the shoot by four, we might still get out before rush hour—they did, but we didn't. The trip was further delayed by a pit stop at a Ninth Avenue bar.

"I'm very thirsty," she said. "You know how it is after a long day." She cocked her head and smiled at me as if I knew.

"Why don't you join me?" she asked.

Teri was a former model and still very beautiful, but all the charm in the world was not going to get me to bring two kids into a sleazy bar. I gestured to the kids in the back seat.

"Oh," she said, "They won't be a problem. Brooke comes with me all the time."

I shook my head. "You go ahead. We'll wait, but I'd like to get out of the city before the rush hour."

I had no idea how I'd gotten myself into the position of sitting in a car waiting for this lady to get out of a bar. Meanwhile, Brooke and Jon had formed a friendship that was good enough to get Jon invited to Brooke's thirteenth birthday party. Unfortunately, it was a pool party, and Jon, who couldn't swim, spent the whole party sitting on the side of the pool like little Alvy Singer in the stockade. He looked longingly at his love, while Brooke and her friends swam around. Had Woody Allen shot the pool party instead of the Thanksgiving play, Brooke might still be in the movie.

We didn't make it home until seven that night. We were exhausted, and Jon had to be back on the set by eight thirty the next morning. They were shooting a scene under the boardwalk in Coney Island. I had had a brief look at the script. It was something about sailors, a pretty girl, and little Alvy Singer taking a condom out of his wallet and watching as it turned to dust. I thought of the scene and began to wonder if I was compromising my kid. Maybe, when it came down to it, I wasn't much better than Teri Shields.

Woody Allen, to his credit, was considerate and respectful of Jonathan's age. Allen walked over to me, explained the scene and asked, "Are you okay with that?"

"Yes, it's fine."

"What shall I tell him it is?" Allen asked.

"Tell him it's an old balloon," I said.

Satisfied. Allen went back on the set and they shot the scene. Jonathan didn't ask any questions.

It was easy to explain the condom to Jon, but I'd no idea how Malle and Teri were going to explain child prostitution to Brooke.

Jonathan finished shooting *Annie Hall* three weeks later than we'd been promised. It took *chutzpah*, but I pulled him off the set so that he could start his new summer camp with the rest of the kids. I'd told the assistant producer from the beginning that Jon would be leaving on June 21, but they'd ignored me and kept writing scenes. I was stuck in one of those dilemmas where I was trying to be true to my kid, but also not wanting to screw up the movie. We found a compromise. I agreed to let them fly Jon back after two weeks, figuring by then he would have settled into camp. Jonathan said he didn't care, because the kids were jerks and he missed his friends on the set. I feared that I had alienated everybody affiliated with the film. I must not have screwed up too badly because they later cast Robert in *Stardust Memories*. They may not have liked me, but they did like my kids.

By that time, the whole *biz* was starting to wind down. After *Annie Hall*, I could tell that Jonathan had had it. Delores sent him up for the lead in *My Bodyguard*, directed by Tony Bill. Coming off the film that won the Oscar for Best Picture, he was a shoo-in for the part until, that is, he told the director that he had had amblyopia and that his eye still, on occasion, wandered all over his face. This of course was no longer true, but it was enough to scare the director and lose him the part.

After *Stardust Memories*, Rob had had it also. It was the repeated takes of the elephant scene on the beach that did it for Rob. He hated being hoisted up on wires. He was frightened. I wasn't on the set that day, but I was told that they had to do a number of takes. I felt terrible. After all my protective efforts, my child still ended up traumatized.

Around that time, David had finished shooting several spots in a series of Honeycomb cereal commercials. Everybody had gotten his turn in front of the camera. They had all gone to summer camp five years in a row. I'd graduated from college and socked money away for their future—it was the perfect time to quit the *biz*.

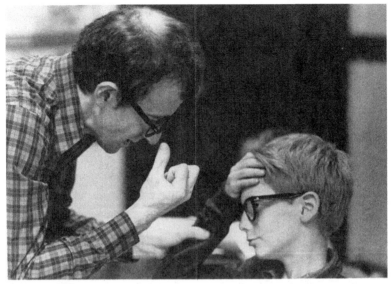

Woody Allen and Jonathan on the set of Annie Hall (1977),
a United Artist release

Little Alvy Singer: scene in doctor's office.

running it over again

The Lindbergh Road, a narrow, sparsely populated ribbon of road where the aviator and his family once lived, serpentines over and through the Sour Grass Mountains. Three times a week, I drove that road to get to my analyst Nancy's office. On this particularly beautiful Monday morning, it had rained during the night, but by the time I got into my car, the sun was peeking through the clouds, reflecting off the wet gravel, and casting striped shadows across the road. Usually when I passed the Lindberg house, I'd look up with morbid fascination, as if I might see the ghost of the kidnapped baby hovering over the stone walls. This time I was in a hurry. Shortly after I'd awoken—lying in that hypnogogic state between sleep and wakefulness—a dream came into my consciousness that had filled me with dread. I was anxious to tell Nancy about it.

I was driving like a racer, accelerating into the curves, slaloming right and left, when a black squirrel ran out in front of the car. I swerved and nearly lost control of the wheel, sure that the thump I had felt was the tire going over the animal. I jammed on the brakes and screeched to a halt—had there been a car anywhere behind me, I'd surely have been rear-ended.

I looked in the rearview mirror, scanning the road behind me, but saw nothing. There was no carcass. Maybe I hadn't hit it after all, yet that thump was unmistakable. My mind raced. What if the animal was caught up in the treads of the tire, and, if I drove away, with each turn of the wheel, I'd be running it over again? I got out of the car and ran around examining the tires, expecting to see a fuzzy tail sticking out from under the fender—there was none. *Well, that's that then.* I got back in the car and started pulling away when a very unsettling thought took root: *What if the injured squirrel had limped to the side of the road and was lying, writhing in a ditch? What then?* I should go over and do the humane thing—hit it on the head with a rock and smash it out of its misery. I felt sick to my stomach and started gulping for air. I was having an anxiety attack. I sat there with my head on the steering wheel till I could get control of my breath, and then I drove off, realizing with self-loathing and great shame that I'd rather have left a small animal to die in agony in a ditch than to be late for my forty-five-minute therapy session.

I hadn't had anxiety attacks since I was twenty years old, when Howard and I moved to Boston. It was the year after we'd married. Howard's job at the time took us to Walpole, Massachusetts—an unremarkable suburb of Boston known for its maximum-security prison. It was a joy to be away from Brooklyn. My mother had a stranglehold on my life, and I'd hoped that the move would get her to loosen her grip, but no sooner had I settled into our new apartment than I started having severe anxiety attacks. I didn't know what they were. I'd start gasping for air, sure that I was dying. A physician checked me out, said I was fine, and referred me to a psychotherapist. *Oh my God*, I thought, *I'm crazy like my mother.*

I put off making the appointment until the morning I started hyperventilating at work and had to hide in a bathroom stall for a half hour until I caught my breath. I sheepishly returned to my desk, picked up the phone, and called the therapist.

His name was Donald Stern—a short Jewish guy with a scruffy beard and an office that I'd later realize he'd modeled after Freud's office in Vienna. Instead of a couch, it had a chaise lounge that was covered with a small Persian rug. Artifacts were scattered around the room. He was telling the world that he was a psychoanalyst, but I was too naive to know what that meant. When he asked me to come three times a week and to lie on the chaise, I figured that he too thought I was crazy. In my own defense, I agreed to once-a-week sessions.

It didn't take Donald long to understand the panic attacks.

"You are having grave doubts about your marriage," he said, "and you are consumed with guilt over your separation from your mother."

Donald's interpretation was right. My mother's suicide threats haunted me—the happier I was being away from her, the guiltier I felt and the more frightened I became.

When he explained what was happening to me, the attacks stopped as precipitously as they had begun. I'd started to trust him and agreed to increase the frequency of the sessions. I even took the risk of telling him about the recurring dream I'd had throughout my adolescence.

Every day after school I had to go to this large, gray, limestone building and enter a room where instruments of torture hung on the walls: leather straps, handcuffs, paddles, etc. I had to select one with which I'd be punished.

When we first started working together and Donald took my history, I'd told him about experimental medical treatments I'd had when I was thirteen.

"When I was three years old," I said, "I had a severe ear infection that burst my eardrum and left me mostly deaf in my left ear. I was staying with my grandmother at the time. Had she called the doctor and had I been given penicillin, it might have been all right, but, like many immigrants, Grandma was intimidated by doctors. She held me to her breast all night. I remember the pain and how I cried."

"Anyway, when I was thirteen, I ended up getting radium treatments to burn out the scar tissue. It was at Columbia Presbyterian Hospital in the Bronx. The doctor said if the radium didn't work, he would operate. Once a week we went up to the hospital, where for one hour I'd lie alone on a table with a stick of radium up my nose and into the middle of my ear. I was repeatedly warned that it would be dangerous if I moved. I stayed stock-still. I don't know how I did it," I told Donald.

"I had thirteen treatments. When they were done, and I still couldn't hear out of my left ear, the treatments were declared a failure, and I was scheduled for surgery. That," I said to Donald, "was another nightmare."

Because I was thirteen, it was uncertain if I should be in the adult or the children's wing. I'm not sure who made the decision, but I was humiliated when I was put on the pediatric floor and when they wheeled me down to surgery, feet hanging off the child-sized gurney—reminding me of when I was too big for my crib. I welcomed the ether.

"You should know," I continued, "the surgery didn't work either. My hearing is still dependent on my ability to read lips and my superior right ear. But mostly what stayed with me from those dark days was my mother's misery at having to get out of bed so early, schlep me from New Jersey to the Bronx, and then sit around for an hour waiting for me to get off the table. I'd lie there, imagining her smoking cigarettes, pacing the floor, looking at her watch, and wishing I'd be done already. Intent on not having her suffer any more than was necessary, I did not complain. I climbed up on the table, lifted my chin, and presented my nose without a whimper."

When we analyzed the dream, it became obvious that the limestone building was Columbia Presbyterian Hospital and that, deep down, I felt less the cooperative child and more like one of Mengele's Holocaust victims—keeping my mouth shut and determined to stay alive. What I'd gone through was torture. And my mother hadn't been forthcoming with anything resembling compassion or maternal support. In fact, I'd worried about her more than myself.

Howard had left Boston, eager to be back in Brooklyn and near his mother. I was living on my own, reveling in the single life. Had I not gotten pregnant and had the Boston Strangler not been creating terror, I might have stayed in Walpole, gotten a divorce, and finished my analysis with Donald. But my mother was calling me every day and railing at me.

"What *kind* of woman are you? You leave your husband to live alone and who knows who he'll hook up with?"

"Ma, who are you talking about, Howard or Dad?"

"Don't start on your father. I'm talking about you."

"Howard's fine on his own," I told her, "and so am I."

When the strangler killed a woman a mile away from my apartment, he gave my mother the ammunition she needed to lure me back.

"It's not just you that you have to think about now—it's your baby. You are responsible for another life. Come home right now."

I very reluctantly left Donald and the small taste I'd had of the single life. I returned to Brooklyn to resume my marriage and have my baby.

It was many years later, when, consumed by guilt over my mother's suicide, I went back into therapy.

Nancy, my analyst, lived in a Federalist house with a red brick façade and wide columns. It looked like the courthouse buildings you see in the center of old New England towns. The entrance to the office was behind the house and up a wooden staircase. Many times, I'd wished that I could have entered through the front door and seen her "personal quarters" but they were off limits, allowing my imagination free rein.

I pictured a dark, wood-paneled Dickensian library with sconces of light illuminating leather-bound books neatly kept in glass cabinets. On Christmas holidays—Nancy was not Jewish—I imagined little children playing under the tree, while friends and family sat around a large mahogany table, laden with ham and turkey and white mounds of mashed potatoes. I pictured myself, shivering in the cold, peering in through the frosted window, hungry for the warmth of the fire and a bite to eat, like the Little Match Girl.

I was, at thirty-eight years old, a divorced mother of three and a full-time graduate student, but when I lay down on Nancy's couch, I regressed to the troubled age of four. My literary references shifted away from Winnicott, Freud, and the other psychology texts, and returned to the Grimm and Anderson fairy tales of my childhood. I was particularly obsessed with stories with rescue themes—Rapunzel, Sleeping Beauty, Cinderella. Heidi had special appeal—the whole idea of adoption was tantalizing, not because I wanted to be adopted, but because I imagined I had been. How was it possible that this man and woman with whom I lived were my real parents? I pretended that at any moment there would be a knock at the door and the original set would appear, see me sitting alone in my room talking to my Tiny Tears doll, grab me by the arm, and yank me into the life I was meant to be living. My parents would be crying as I left, bereft over what they had lost.

The end of each therapy session was so wrenching that I suggested taking up residency in Nancy's attic or, even more fancifully, that I simply become lint in her pocket.

"You wouldn't even know I was there," I said.

These pathetic supplications stand as testimony to my desperation at that time.

I never would have thought I could become so dependent on a blonde, blue-eyed *shiksa* who dressed like a Bryn Mawr coed. After Donald, I'd wished for a *haimisheh*, grandmotherly type who would ladle out wisdom like chicken soup. How, I'd wondered, would a nice Protestant woman ever understand the depth of my Jewish guilt? Had she not come so highly recommended, I would have shaken her hand and run out the door, but I was in bad shape and needed help.

The very first session, in rushed and pressured speech, I put it all right out on the table, and waited to see how she'd react.

"I assisted in my mother's suicide," I told her. "That might sound like hyperbole to you, but it's not to me. I know I didn't pour the pills down her throat, but I might as well have handed her the bottle. Don't even try to tell me that I didn't push her hand, because I won't believe you. Don't tell me that if she hadn't killed herself that day, she would have killed herself the day after, because the truth is you *don't* really know that. You *don't* really know that," I reiterated. "At age fifty-two she was dead. She left me three things: five hundred dollars in a sugar bowl, which I gave to my husband Howard to buy a suit for the funeral; a diamond ring, which I stuck in a drawer; and a suicide note that read 'You have Howard, Grandma has Sam, and I have no one.'"

"And," my analyst added. "She also left you a legacy of guilt."

"Right."

Nancy didn't flinch. I heard no platitudes or recriminations. And so we began. . . . She may not have been a Jew but she was a *mensch*, and for years she worked assiduously to find mitigating circumstances that would help disavow me of the belief that I had assisted in my mother's murder. Nothing seemed to work until the day I killed the squirrel and remembered the dream.

I came running in the door just as the previous patient was descending the stairs. Psychoanalytic protocol suggests that one patient be respectful of the other's privacy and avoid eye contact. I was too upset to care. I stared him right in the eye.

He tried to avoid my gaze, but I wasn't having it. He was an interloper, a pretender to my throne. He might as well know, then and there, who was the favored patient and whose couch he'd been warming.

There was a fire burning in the potbelly stove that stood in the corner of the office. It flickered light off the ceiling and cast soft shadows on the wood that paneled the walls. The blinds closed out the sun, and, although the room was warm, I was still chilled to the bone. A plaid blanket was folded at the end of the couch. I pulled it up to my neck and waited for Nancy to grab her notebook and settle back into the recliner—the cue that she was ready to start.

I had imbued Nancy with the heart of a saint. She would never in a million years let a squirrel die alone in a ditch. I was too ashamed to tell her what I had done. I began the session instead with a funny incident that had happened during the week.

"I was doing a practicum on the Emergency Psychiatric Service. Remember the woman I told you about who came in in an acute erotic psychosis? She got up on the table in the waiting room and began to strip."

"I'm not sure," she said.

"Oh, come on, Nancy. Don't you remember how Dr. Jones couldn't talk her down, and how she grabbed his tie and pulled him close to her? All the interns were watching in fascination as he tried to unfurl her from his body."

"Yes, I recall that story now," she said, laughing.

"Well, I had a funny incident also. I was on duty Thursday night and they brought in a big, maybe six foot, four inch tall, African American prisoner from the county jail. The man was incarcerated, awaiting arraignment. They had stuck him in a cell with a bunch of guys, none of whom you'd want to invite home to dinner, and he went into a homosexual panic.

"The guard who brought him in stayed outside the door while I did the evaluation. It was my job to decide if he was suicidal and needed to be committed or if he was fit to await his arraignment. We were in a cement, windowless room the size of a closet. It was hard to keep our knees from touching.

"I started the mental status. I was having trouble getting him to focus on the questions until I tested him for his ability to comprehend metaphor. 'What does this mean?' I asked. 'A bird in the hand is worth two in the bush?'

"His eyes darted around. 'You look here, lady,' he said. 'I don't know why you're talking about your bush. I ain't going anywhere near your bush. Where's the officer? Get me out of here. You're crazy!' he yelled."

I laughed, Nancy laughed, and then, out of the blue, I started to cry. I had no conscious awareness that the stories I'd been relating about inappropriate sexual behavior were connected to the dream I hadn't yet remembered to tell.

I kept picturing the squirrel, wondering if it was still writhing in the ditch or if it was already dead. I wondered if a hawk spotted it and started to eat it before it was even dead. My thoughts got more and more grotesque. I realized that I had to tell her what I had done, even if it meant her condemnation.

"I mangled a squirrel and left it to die on the side of a lonely road. I felt the thump under the wheels."

"Did you see the carcass?" she asked.

"No, but I heard the thump. I think it must have limped off into a ditch. I just left it there," I sobbed. "I left it to die alone in a ditch."

"You don't know that," she countered. "You can't be sure you hit it."

"I didn't see my mother's corpse either," I said annoyed, "so I suppose I couldn't know for sure if it was she who was buried that day."

"How quickly you associate to your mother," Nancy said.

"Yeah, well, except I didn't wish the squirrel dead."

"You did not wish your mother dead, either," she said. "You wished her to be well and to let you be your own woman."

"Yes," I answered, "but given that I knew the latter was impossible, the former must be true."

"You know," she said, "the squirrel need not just represent your mother, it could also represent you. I'm thinking about those radium treatments you had as a child—when you were left to lie alone on a table with a stick up your nose."

It was then that I'd remembered the dream.

"I had a dream," I said.

I am four, maybe, five years old. It is the morning. I am standing barefoot in the corner of Grandma's kitchen. I have slept over at Grandma's house again. The linoleum is cold, but the heat from the radiator brushes my nightgown and warms my back. Grandma is in the bedroom making the bed. My mother has come to pick me up and take me home. I am upset, trying to tell her something important about my grandfather. "I have a secret. Grandpa and I took a nap together. He held me funny." As I began to elaborate, she clasped her hand over my mouth and glared at me. What have I done? I must have done something very, very bad. "Shush," she warned. "Do you hear me, Linda? Do not tell your grandmother or anybody else. It's a secret." She gritted her teeth. The words spit out of her mouth. "Do you hear me?" she hissed. I looked at her face and suddenly I realized that she knew what I was going to tell her, and that to tell my secret was to give hers away.

I was sobbing. I forced myself to take a deep breath. Another. Another. Minutes passed.

"What do you make of the dream?" Nancy asked. "It is unusual for a dream. It is not scrambled or disguised. It seems more like a memory than a dream."

"It's just a dream," I insisted.

"Maybe not. Memories can be disguised as dreams."

"Yes," I said, annoyed, "but dreams misinterpreted as memories can also be lies."

"Perhaps you and your mother had the same secret. You were warned not to tell your grandmother but you can tell it to me," she said.

"Tell you what? I have no secret. It was just a dream."

I left the session, certain Nancy was making something out of nothing.

As I drove home, my mood began to lift. When I got to the curve where I'd hit the squirrel, I slowed down and looked again for the carcass—nothing. I pulled the car over to the side of the road, got out and examined the ditch. There was no squirrel. Maybe I hadn't hit it at all.

I got back in the car and continued to drive. There is a hairpin turn where the road leaves the woods and opens to farmland. I pulled over and stopped the car. The field was blanketed with yellow flowers from the rapeseed plant. Mozart's Clarinet Concerto was playing on the radio. A hawk, catching thermals, danced to the music.

the hand off

Every weekend, my ninety-two-year-old father, George, checked into the hospital emergency room, not because he was sick, but because the food was good, and he liked the company. He referred to the nurses and the doctors as his "staff," conjuring one ailment or another and showing up every Friday night. Sometimes he'd fiddle with his medications to throw off his heart rhythm, arriving at the ER pale and bloodless. Other times, inflated with his own bluster, he'd be flushed, but there was nothing wrong with my father that couldn't be cured by having a lady to hug and some money to burn.

I never got used to the "He's here again" phone call from the emergency room nurse. My second husband, also named George, had died the year before. I was trying to adapt to being on my own and taking care of myself, but my father's antics didn't give me much of an opportunity. I was a psychologist with a busy private practice, but I'd drop whatever it was I should have been doing and run over to the hospital. By the time I'd get there, he would have regained his normal color. He'd admonish me, but not really, for rushing to his bedside, and then happily announce that the doctors wanted to keep him overnight for a little observation.

He kept the blue curtain around his bed open so he could survey his kingdom and watch the comings and goings of his *staff*. My father always knew how to sidle up to whomever he thought might matter and make them feel as if they actually did.

When the nurses came into his cubicle, he'd have them bend over so he could read their nametags and look at their cleavage. He'd summon the doctors by their first names. When his dinner tray came, he'd send it back if the chicken was too dry or the soup wasn't hot enough. No one seemed to know quite what to do about him. He was jovial. He made them laugh. At times, they looked exasperated, but I could tell that they were also charmed. My father had always been a player, and, at ninety-two, he still knew how to shuffle the deck and pull out the joker. By Sunday night, when the doctors concluded that nothing was wrong, he would get up, get dressed, order his car, tip the valet at the hospital door, and drive himself home.

Throughout my life, whenever my father "needed" me, I'd run to his side. This was not a normal father-daughter obligation; it was servitude with a smile. My indenture began at birth. I was conceived for the express job of keeping my father out of the army. Before I was born, the draft board declared my father 4F. At minus three months, I had already failed to achieve my intended purpose. I was like the kid who flunked out of college but was still stuck with the student loans.

My mother and father had different ways of calling in their chits. My mother conscripted me immediately—lifetime employment with no benefits that I could see. Along with being the draw for my father, I was to be her confidante, best friend, and marriage counselor. This entailed a myriad of duties, none of which were appropriate for a child. I was to listen to secrets about my father's infidelities, to always take her side, and intervene with my father as the situation required. My labors on her behalf were fruitless, given his proclivities and the fact that she didn't stop nagging him for one second.

My father—having no instincts for parenthood and recognizing my mother's plan for me—responded by ignoring both of us. He stayed away from the house as much as possible and, when he came home, hid behind the newspaper. He sat in his chair, the smoke from his cigar wafting up from behind his paper. When he came to the table, the paper came with him. My mother was a pressure cooker; by the time we got to the dessert, she was ready to blow. I did what had to be done—spilled my milk or fell out of my chair, whatever it took to deflect her rage. My father gave me a smile of appreciation for my sacrifice, and went back to reading *The Daily Mirror* about the Brooklyn Dodgers, J. Edgar Hoover, or whatever was the news of the day.

My father's childhood deprivation became the rationale for his entitlement. He was a good-looking guy. Had he looked like the average Joe, he might've stopped trying to make it big and been satisfied with making it at all. But my father wasn't willing to settle for "small potatoes." With money that came from who knew where, he started a series of manufacturing businesses: handbags, ladies' underwear, and women's hosiery. He usually went from riches to rags within three years, tops.

When he went bankrupt, and he *always* went bankrupt, it was never his fault. His partners were jerks; the factors (the middleman between the banks and the manufacturer) were *ganefs*, thieves; and his wife, well his wife—if she'd only stopped her incessant nagging and supported him just once in her life, his current *situation* wouldn't have occurred. This last remark was a call to arms, and the battle would begin. It didn't matter that they were climbing the same hill over and over again or that I was in the line of fire—there is always some collateral damage in a war. Here's the fight:

"Don't listen to him," she'd start. "I support him plenty. Ask him how much I borrowed from my brothers on his behalf, like they have it to give? Why did I borrow it? Ask him why I borrowed it, Linda, go on ask him."

Hearing my cue, I'd look up from my Nancy Drew mystery. "Why did she borrow the money?" I'd ask. He would keep reading his paper. I'd go back to my mystery.

"I'll tell you why I borrowed it," she'd say, her voice raised by an octave. "I borrowed it so they wouldn't put your father in jail!"

That would always get his attention. He'd throw down the paper in disgust.

"What's the matter with you, Tessie? What are you telling the kid? Linda, don't listen to your mother. She doesn't know what she's talking about. No one gave me nothin'!" he'd shout. "You don't know what you're talking about. How many times do I have to tell you, your brothers didn't give me a loan—they made an *investment*."

Then he'd turn his back to her and look at me. "I don't know what she's talking about. They made an investment. I gave her brothers a chance to make a lot of money. It didn't work out. If it had worked out, they'd be rich, and your father would be a hero. It didn't work out, so now I'm the bad guy. You make an investment, you take a chance." He'd slam his fist on the table, and the lamp would shake.

"An investment? What are you talking, an investment?" she'd yell. "By you, it's not an investment, it's a donation!" Then finally she'd scream, "You'll be happy when I'm six feet under!"

She would storm out of the room; he, out of the house.

I never would have admitted this to my mother, but I was dubious about my father's monetary intentions. I had been robbed at age five. Someone broke into my cash register bank and stole thirty-five dollars out of the cash drawer. This was hard-earned money. I earned this money by putting up with stranglehold hugs from my grandfather. He'd give me a dollar for endurance, and I'd put it in my bank. I ran to my mother back then, to tell her that we'd been robbed.

"You're telling me," was all she said.

On one of my father's weekend forays to the emergency room, he was actually admitted and given a bed on the floor. The doctors were less cavalier this time and said it would be a good idea if I stuck around. I sat by his bedside for hours. Around one in the morning, he came out of his stupor, sat straight up in bed, and declared that he wasn't going to die. I figured this was probably true, as his color had come back, his voice was strong, and besides, I don't know that he ever did anything he didn't want to do.

I'd been playing around with the idea of asking him a question I'd always wondered about, but never had the guts to ask. I figured now was as good a time as any.

"Do I have any siblings?" I blurted out.

"What, are you kidding me?" He looked at me like I was crazy.

"It's a legitimate question," I defended.

"That's very funny, you ask a legitimate question about illegitimacy. You're a funny kid. Ask me something else."

"Okay," I said, while the nurse took his blood. "What was the best time of your life?" He thought a moment.

"You want to know? I'll tell you. The best time of my life was when I was president of the Amboy Dukes."

"President? When were you president?"

"What's the difference when I was president, I was president. We had red satin jackets with 'Amboy Dukes' and our names written in gold across the back. Mine said, 'President.'"

I couldn't tell if he was making a fashion statement or bragging about his status.

Here's how I'd first found out about the Amboy Dukes:

It's 1970. I'm twenty-eight. My father is fifty-three. My father changes his shirt at my mother's shiva, and I see this ugly looking mole on his back. I beg him to go to the doctor, and he resists, but finally he goes. He has a malignant melanoma. They operate immediately and the operation is successful. As he's recovering in the hospital, I'm shaken by the strange realization that my mother's death has saved my father's life. He would never have gone to the doctor without my bugging him, and I would never have seen the mole if we hadn't been sitting *shiva*. She could have been the bereaved widow instead of the lunatic wife. All sympathy would have been with her. All I could think was that this may have been the only bitter pill she didn't get to swallow.

I go to visit him in the hospital after the operation, and he introduces me to Marge the mistress. I recognize her as pink angora from years ago at Longchamps. She's about half his age, give or take, with orange hair and red lipstick. This time she's wearing a lavender angora sweater. She's pretty. They hold hands and smile. I stare in disbelief: my mother's dead two weeks, and he introduces me to his mistress? *Chutzpah* isn't even the word. Everything my mother said, his running around with other women, was true. I felt like I had been harboring a felon, aiding and abetting a criminal, but he'd had cancer; he might die. I remind myself that I'd supported their separation and that I'd rooted for him to have a better life. *Well, he does*, I thought. *Yes, but I had betrayed her.*

The nurse comes in to change his dressing. Marge takes me out into the hall, mutters condolences about my mother, and then, in a lame effort to engage me, she asks, "Did you know that your dad was a member of the Amboy Dukes?"

"What's an Amboy Duke?"

"It was a cellar club in Brownsville," she says. "You know, the gang Irving Shulman wrote the book about."

"I don't know the book. When did it come out?" I hate to indulge her, but by now, I am curious.

"Nineteen forty-seven."

"I was five in nineteen forty-seven."

"Yeah, me too," she says. *Oh great!* "I thought you might have heard about it."

She smiles, raises her eyebrow, and gives me a smile that says *I knew and you didn't*. I am trying to like her for my father's sake, but she's starting out at zero and losing ground fast.

After I leave my father and Marge at the hospital, I go to the library and look up *The Amboy Dukes*. The Dukes were named after Amboy Street, a few blocks from where my father grew up. Irving Shulman's novel was a tawdry bestseller, considered soft porn at the time. It's a misogynistic tale of rape and murder by teenage hoods, sons of immigrants, who, unsupervised, ran the streets of Brownsville Brooklyn. By *Fifty Shades of Grey* standards, *tawdry* would have been a grand overstatement, but, back then, it was a must-read for every horny adolescent.

Years after my father died, I learned that the Amboy Dukes was a feeder gang to Murder Incorporated, aka the Brownsville Boys. Not just in Shulman's novel, but for real. Murder Incorporated was the "enforcement arm" of the Jewish Mafia in the 1930s and 1940s. Read *Tough Jews* by Rich Cohen. It's right in there, about how boys from the Amboy Dukes were recruited by Abe "Kid Twist" Reles and Louis Lepke to carry out their dirty business. I don't know about Dad and Murder Incorporated. All I can tell you is that whenever we went through airport security, he started to sweat, held his arms straight up, and turned to face the wall.

In a pretense of caring and a feeble attempt at protocol, my father waited exactly one year to the day of my mother's death before he married Marge. Aunt Laura said there was no way she was going to watch her brother marry a call girl. She said that her brother was an idiot, and my mother . . . "well, your poor mother," was all she could mutter. Two years after they married, they divorced. This was not a surprise, as Marge thought she was getting a big shot, and he thought he was getting eternal youth. I was in the process of getting divorced myself and struggling to balance my new life. There was no money. I'd taken out loans to pay for college. My father, having been kicked out of her house, asked if he could move in with me for a while. Was I supposed to say no?

Tired now of trying to convince my father that the hospital is not a spa, I got up to leave.

"Sit," he said. "I have something to tell you. I've never told you this. . . ."

"I'm sitting. What?"

"Do you remember when you handed off the money?"

"What are you talking about?'

"I'm talking about when you handed off the money. Your mother knew. I wouldn't have told her, but I needed to borrow you for a day."

"Borrow me . . ."

"I had no choice," he continued. "You had to help your father out."

"What? When? How old was I?" I didn't know what to ask first.

"You were four."

"I was four? I'm four years old, and I'm handing off the money? To whom?" By now he was no longer looking me in the eye. He rang for the nurse. He decided he was hungry, and he wasn't going to talk until he ate his dinner.

They brought him his dinner.

"What are you looking at me for?" he asked, pleased that he had my full attention.

"Just tell me what you're talking about, *please.*"

"It was nothing. We needed to give over some money to the other guys. It wasn't safe, so I needed your help."

"I was only four!" I was incredulous. "How could you get me involved?"

"Don't worry," he said, "we tied a rope around your waist so we could pull you back if they tried to snatch you. What, you think I wouldn't protect you? I'm your father. What's the matter with you? After you handed it off, we took you up to the Laurel-in-the-Pines Hotel for two weeks until the heat died down. We were worried they might kidnap you."

"This is preposterous!! I don't believe—"

"Go to my apartment. Go in the box on the top shelf of the hall closet. There are a couple of pictures from the hotel. Your mother doesn't look too happy. She had to stay alone with you for the second week. We still didn't think it was safe, and I had to get back to New York. Go get the pictures. I'm going to sleep." He turned over and that was that.

The Laurel-in-the-Pines Hotel in Lakewood, New Jersey, was the place to go in the '40s if you were rich and famous, or, as the case seems to have been, infamous. It was what Grandma would have called "fancy schmancy." An all-year-round resort; in the winter they had horse-drawn sleighs. I remember going on a sleigh ride, tucked in a big warm blanket. The bells on the horses' bridles jingled. The sleigh pulled us into the woods. I could smell the pine. The bows were heavy with snow. This was the closest I ever got to the Currier and Ives childhood of my dreams.

On the next page are the two pictures I found in my father's closet.

I'm the cute little kid with the leopard-collar coat. I remember it came with a matching leopard muff. I think I lost the muff. My mother is standing next to me. I can't tell if she's scared or if she's cold, but her smile looks frozen. According to my father, the man standing next to her is the big honcho. He wouldn't tell me his name, so I can't tell you who he is. I don't know if he was being secretive or he just couldn't remember. If it's the latter, then as far as I'm concerned, it makes the whole story suspect. Until, that is, you take a look at the first picture. Now, that's not a group of average Joes! I particularly like the

The Gangsters

Linda, mother, and gangster at
the Laurel-in-the-Pines Hotel

guy on the right with the Jimmy Durante nose. If he wasn't a gangster in real life, he could easily be cast as one in a movie. The little guy in the back with the smile, desperately trying to get into the picture, is my father.

I've tried to conjure up the handoff so many times that I can no longer tell if it's my imagination or a real memory. But here is one more piece of information to consider: my uncle Harry loved to regale me with stories of my father's exploits. If you ask me, my uncle, always having lived on the straight and narrow, got a kick out of my father. When he told the stories, he sounded like he was bragging about the exploits of an adolescent son. One of his favorite stories was the one about the money in the vault. He particularly liked to tell it when I was present so I could recite my lines. My uncle, who went to City College and had perfect English, always told the story with an accent like a tough guy who was a dropout from Thomas Jefferson High School.

"I come home on leave from the army . . . you know your father was 4F?" he would begin.

"Don't remind me," I'd say.

"Yeah, well I come home on leave, and your father says, 'Come with me.' He takes me to a bank. Opens a vault. What do you think is in the vault?"

I answer with mock surprise, "The money?"

"Right," he confirms. "I ask him, 'Georgie, what are you doing with this money?' I don't believe what I'm seeing. 'How much do you have here?'

"'Count it,' he tells me. I count it. You wouldn't believe . . . he has a hundred thousand dollars sitting in that vault. Linda, do you *know* how much money a hundred thousand dollars was back then?"

"A million dollars," I say on cue.

"That's right." A pause for effect. "A million dollars." He smiles. "I'm telling you, your father opens this goddamn vault and shows me a million dollars. Can you believe . . . ?" This is where Uncle Harry laughs with delight. "A million goddamn dollars. I ask, 'Where the hell did you get this money?' You know what he tells me? The black market. Which black market? What black market? I want to know what the hell he's been doing. He tells me it don't matter; he has to give it back anyway. 'To who?' I ask. He don't tell me. He shows me all this money—tells me nothin'. That's your father! I tell him to put some away for Linda's college. Did he put it away? *No*. Did your father ever listen to me? *No*. If he'd listened to me . . ." And here, Uncle Harry goes off on a riff about his own accomplishments.

After I went to my father's apartment, found the pictures in the closet, and came back to the hospital, I told him in no uncertain terms that I no longer felt guilty for my existence. That it seems like I came in handy after all.

"What do you mean, handy?" he wanted to know. "You always came in handy. I don't know what you're talking about," he said. "Do me a favor. Call the valet and tell them to get my car ready."

My husband George

⟡ my name is linda ⟡

The first time we went away with all five kids, George had rented a house on the beach on Fire Island. There is a picture of me sitting on the back steps. I'm in my nightgown, wearing George's sweatshirt and holding a mug of coffee. I look like I'm posed for an ad, but it isn't clear what I'm selling. I remember the smell of the salt air, the caw of the gulls, and the sound of the waves slapping on the shore. I was thirty-five with three little kids, and so much in love that I let the red flags fly in the wind and just enjoyed the breeze.

It took George five years to ask me to marry him, which I thought was four too many. His proposal, when it did come, was more an explanation of benefits than a declaration of love. "You need health insurance, so we might as well," he said.

I squelched my longing for a more touching expression of his devotion and desire and immediately answered, "Yes."

He wanted a small, unassuming wedding, so we had the ceremony at the Rutgers chapel—I was in school there at the time, so the chapel was free. I wore a white suit with a pencil skirt and fitted jacket, something my mother would have approved of, or even worn herself. In the picture from the wedding, I'm standing under the *chuppa*. I am as thin as a shadow.

I had only gotten out of the hospital two weeks before. Once each semester, because of scar tissue from an earlier surgery, my intestines tied up in a knot. I'd lie in a bed for a week with a tube down my nose into my stomach, and an IV in my arm, an intervention intended to relieve my stomach of its usual function, until it untwisted enough to do the job for which it was intended. Thirsty for real drink, I'd hallucinate egg creams and malteds while I waited until I could swallow food again. It was a forced vacation with no expectations and a relief from being on my own, taking care of the kids and the house, going to school three nights a week, and running back and forth to the city for auditions, but it left me weak and shaky.

I was happy that George took charge of the wedding arrangements except for his decision that we marry on December 18th. I reminded him that date had already been claimed by my mother. I could not possibly marry on the anniversary of her suicide. George acquiesced and we set the date for December 17th instead. It was still closer then I would have liked but I was afraid to rock the boat so I let it go. He booked The Wooden Nickel, a neighborhood restaurant, for the luncheon reception. I chose to ignore the metaphor, and when he told me I simply said, "Fine." We were twenty people in a small room with a long table; Grandma sat at one end, trying not to look at my father sitting with his new bride—the man and the woman she held responsible for her daughter's suicide. It was a testament to Grandma's love that she came at all, but she brought my mother's ghost with her—an eerie presence that haunted the day.

Before we married, I had tried to convince George that we should sell both our houses and start fresh in a neutral residence, where the kids and I wouldn't feel like trespassers, and he and his kids wouldn't feel like they were being invaded.

George wasn't having it. He said if I gave him the money I realized after the sale of my house—half went to Howard—he would add on extra rooms to accommodate us. As a consolation, he converted the poolroom that he had constructed for his sons, complete with swinging bar doors and Willy Nelson music, back into the living room it was meant to be.

Despite the renovations, it was still the house he'd owned with his ex-wife, Barbara. She still had a key and squatting rights. Every Thursday afternoon she would open the door, walk in, and plop herself down on the easy chair in the den, where she would sit like a sentry and wait for her two children to emerge from their rooms to "spend quality time with their mother." Most of the time, it was my son David who kept her company.

When I balked at the intrusion, George patiently explained that the arrangement was part of their custody agreement, and didn't I want his kids to maintain a relationship with their mother?

Our money arrangement was also strange. The minimal amount Howard paid in child support became my allowance. It was meant to cover my personal needs—college tuition, clothes and sundries, haircuts. I had a separate telephone number so we could keep track of my phone expenses. Everything else required his okay. George was paying for all of my children's expenses, so on what grounds could I possibly complain? *And wasn't he as rigid with himself as he was with me? Didn't he write separate checks for every charge he made?* When the bill came, he'd stuff the envelope with all the checks and mail it off.

I thought all of this was a little crazy, but convinced myself that he would loosen up once I opened my practice and started contributing to the coffers—then money would no longer be the currency of our relationship, and we would achieve the closeness I longed for. In the meantime, I felt like a puppy in a crate—cute, but likely to chew on the furniture and mess up the rug. I was frustrated, but for the most part I cooperated. Until the wallpaper in our bedroom became the tipping point.

"Did you notice, dear, in the mornings when the light comes through the blinds, how the gray stripes on the paper look like bars in a prison cell?" I asked.

"No," he said, "I didn't notice. It's new wallpaper. Barbara redid the bedroom just before we separated. It looks fine to me."

If Barbara's decorating taste was dictated by her state of mind, then she and I had more in common than just having married the same man. I kept that thought to myself.

Once I'd seen the bars, they wouldn't go away, and each morning they became more pronounced.

After two months of unanswered pleas, and on a day when no one was home, I went to the hardware store, rented a steamer, and carefully steamed every bar off the walls. Like peeling strips of dead skin off a sunburned arm, I delighted in lifting each panel of the wretched paper. When I was done, and the rough wallboard was exposed, I took purple and yellow magic markers and drew large, wild, forget-me-not flowers. Across the stems and in scrawling script I wrote, My Name Is Linda.

I poured a glass of red wine, perched in the middle of the bed and waited with pride and fear for George to come home and see my handiwork. I heard the car pull up in the driveway.

"Lin," he called.

"In here," I yelled, splashing the wine on the bed.

He walked in, saw the walls, and said, "What the hell? What am I supposed to say, Linda?"

"You could say 'Thank you.'"

He shook his head and left the room. I heard his briefcase slam down on the kitchen counter. The next morning when I awoke, the bars were gone, the sun cast shadows on beautiful purple and yellow flowers, and George still slept beside me. I was triumphant.

Two weeks later I got his permission to repaper the walls. I picked a Ralph Lauren paisley print and bought a new duvet. He stubbornly would not admit he liked the change.

Later, when I read Charlotte Perkins Gilman's quintessential feminist story, "The Yellow Wallpaper," I would realize that I was not the first woman to experience the wallpaper phenomenon.

The need to sign my artwork and declare my identity had been instigated by two prior events, my first Director's Council trip to Puerto Rico shortly after George and I had met, and my father's precipitous name change when I was a teenager.

The Director's Council was a company perk for big producers. The packet for the trip had come in the mail before we left. Enclosed were two nametags—GEORGE and BARBARA. George, not trusting his rightful membership in the Council—for reasons that I would only understand later—insisted we adhere to the company rules of propriety. He was afraid of being ousted.

"I'm technically still married," he said.

"I'm technically not Barbara," I said.

He hung the nametag around my neck, like a lei around a winning horse. I spent our time in Puerto Rico trying to remember to answer to my nametag name. *Wasn't it worth it to be on a beautiful island with my beloved?* I asked myself. *And hadn't I on my honeymoon with Howard, paraded around an entire week answering to my new married name—a name that never in twelve years sounded right? So I was Barbara for three days. So what was the big deal?*

When I was in high school, my father—without consultation, overnight—changed our last name from Meyerowitz to Meyers. My mother figured he was running from the mob or the taxman. I figured he was running from my mother.

"What does this mean?" I asked. "Should I drop the 'owitz' when I sign my name?"

"Go ask your father," she said.

"Where is he?"

"I should know?"

I dropped the "owitz" then, and, later, when I divorced Howard, I went back to Meyers. When I married George, I stuck with Meyers. Though everything else in my life had changed, at least my name was the same, but inside I suffered an identity crisis.

Three times a week I lay on my analyst's couch, searching for an ego.

"Who am I?" I asked.

"Who do you want to be?" she answered.

"A partner with the man I love and a strong, independent woman."

The women in my consciousness-raising group weren't so sure I was on the right path. Sarah Schatz and Joyce Goldenberg had applauded the wallpaper action, but were gravely disturbed by the earlier nametag situation. I was called a traitor to the feminist cause. It was whispered that I should be asked to leave the group. Sarah Schatz stood up for me and said that my errant behavior was proof that I needed the group most of all. I remained, but I complained.

"You don't understand love," I said.

"You're trading self for love," someone said.

"No, I'm enhancing self with love," I said.

Whenever I began a sentence with *George says*, I'd be interrupted.

"What do *you* say?" they'd ask.

That question flummoxed me, too—somewhere between the first date and the marriage, I had lost my own opinion.

I put myself on fast forward and got my doctorate in clinical psychology in four years. I threw myself a big party at the house. Family, friends, and colleagues joined me in celebration. George gave me a kiss and a beautiful butterfly pin with gold wings. He was clearly proud of my accomplishment. My father gave me a hug, clinked a glass for attention, held up my arm in a triumphant salute.

"My son, the doctor," he proudly announced.

Etienne, a fellow psych intern, having just met my husband and my father, took me aside and in an audible whisper said, "You're living proof of the Oedipus conflict. Freud's smiling in his grave. I mean look at them—both named George and they look like brothers. What's the age difference between your father and George?"

"Nine years," I muttered.

"And fifteen years between you and your husband, right?"

"Yeah, so?"

"So, nothing. Just saying."

Pompous little prick. I knew I shouldn't have invited him. I walked away questioning if analysis three times a week was going to be enough.

I opened an office on Nassau Street in Princeton—an old building populated with therapists. The office had a non-working fireplace—no fire, but it gave the room a lovely ambiance. I painted the woodwork a dark green and put up camel-colored wallpaper. When done, the room was stately and gave off an air of professional confidence I had yet to feel.

It didn't take long for me to have a full practice and a good income. I refused George's allowance and started paying my own way. The more money I earned, the more *chutzpah* I got.

On a Sunday when George came home, happy from his success on the paddleball court, I handed him a cup of coffee, leaned over, and gave him a kiss.

"What's up?" he asked.

"It's time to move," I said. "I want to move to Princeton."

"Come on, Lin, don't start. This house is fine. What do we have to move for? Each of the kids has their own room. You've repapered our bedroom."

"The kids are out of the house, and no matter what I've done to fix it up, it will always be your house with Barbara. I want us to start fresh. Please," I said.

"I'll think about it."

"For how long?" I asked.

"I don't know. I'll think about it. Don't push me." He put the cup down and walked out of the kitchen.

Weeks went by and he said nothing. I went to a realtor on my own and found a hundred-year-old colonial in Princeton—a quirky house, turned around on the property, the back of the house facing the street. The garden had pink rhododendrons as high as the first-floor windows, a wisteria vine so old and twisted that it had strangled the arbor it rested on. In June, a canopy of lavender blossoms crisscrossed the boughs of the trees, and a gnarled magnolia stood at the corner of the picket fence. I wished I'd grown up in this house.

"You're going to love it," I promised. "At least come look."

George walked through the rooms, his eyes darting from one potential problem to another.

"It's beautiful isn't it?" I prompted.

"It's going to need a lot of work," he said.

"But first tell me if you like it," I said.

"It's going to be a fortune. Where's the money supposed to come from?"

"The stock market's been good. I'm earning. We can do it. I promise."

Arm in arm, we walked around the neighborhood. George's mouth was tight as he chewed on his mustache.

"What's wrong?" I asked.

"I like every house I see," he said.

"That's great. Isn't that great?"

"No it's not. The neighborhood is too rich," he said.

"Too rich for what?" I asked.

"Too rich for me," he answered.

"George, we can afford this house," I said. "You'll see how it will become a fit. Just give it a chance."

I didn't know till the last minute if George was going to go through with the sale. I knew by the arm he put around my shoulders and the hand that stroked my back that he wanted to please me, but he was frightened. For a man who only bought two-year-old Cadillacs—a compromise between his wish to both display and disguise his entitlement and his wealth—moving to Princeton was like sporting a brand new car. He sat across the table from the seller and the lawyers like a felon before a judge. In the end, he signed the contract, and we got the deed. He quickly took the papers, put them in his brief-case, shook hands all around, and led me out of the office.

"Let's go celebrate. Come on," I urged. "You can get a Black Russian and I'll get a martini. We'll toast a new beginning," I said.

"The money is about to run out on the meter," he said, "and I have to get back to the office."

George's house was on the market for three months, but there had been no bids. The realtor said he'd priced it too high. The real estate market was dropping, but George had a number in his head and he wasn't willing to let go. When I tried to shake him loose, he growled and snapped at me.

"If you would adjust to the market and lower the price, the house would sell," I said.

"Don't tell me what to do with my house," he said.

"Thank you. You just made my point. It was not *our* house—it was *never* our house and that is exactly why we needed to move."

I was very sad when George wouldn't join me in decorating the new house. I took the money I was earning and did it myself. I turned the living room into a library, with built-in book-shelves and two small couches facing each other on either side of the fireplace. I saved us having to renovate the old kitchen by painting the cabinets white, buying new hardware, and stenciling the old wooden floor. George had once said he wanted a black bedroom. I found wallpaper with large red roses on a black background. I bought a black quilt and black pillow shams. He perked up when it came time to decorate his study. He put in a daybed, a television, and a desk. It was spare, but he liked it. I knew he was happy with the job I had done by the way he showed guests around the house.

I saved rent and gained us a tax deduction by moving my office from Nassau Street into the house. It was a beautiful setup. Patients walked up a flagstone path onto the terrace and into a sunlit garden room with a straw rug and wicker furniture. Curtained French doors blocked off the waiting room from the rest of the house. My office, off the garden room, had a gas fireplace rimmed with old Dutch tiles, pine wood paneling, and built-in bookshelves. Patients lying on the couch looked up at a peaked ceiling with exposed beams, painted in a quiet William Morris pattern. Sometimes I wondered if they came to see me, or to simply rest in the warmth of the room.

George was happy in Princeton, as I knew he would be. We went to the Princeton football games and to the plays at McCarter Theater, but something was wrong. He was surly and hard to live with. I was tired from long days in the office and short on patience. Our squabbles had become fights—angry voices, slamming doors. I was told he bragged about me behind my back, but, to my face, he minimized every contribution I made.

"You're not putting in as much as you think," he'd say. "I'm still paying your taxes."

"But I'm also paying Rob's tuition at Lawrenceville," I said.

"I'm still paying your taxes," he reiterated.

I thought that if I opened my own brokerage account he would take me seriously.

"Buy Exxon." he'd call and say.

"Why? What are the upside potential and the downside risks of Exxon these days?" I asked.

"Just buy it," he said. "I wouldn't recommend it if it wasn't a good idea."

"Yes, but I need to know why you're recommending it now," I said.

"You know, Linda, you're a pain in the ass. I don't have time for this. Do as I say or don't, but time is money and I don't have the time," he said.

Most of George's clients did what he told them to do with no questions asked, but I was no longer a *yes* girl. I severed our business relationship in the service of our marriage and my savings—I found a female broker who took the time to explain her recommendations. I began to pick my own stocks and oversee my own account. George became more remote. The further he backed away, the harder I leaned in. It was a tango, without the sex and without the music.

"Why do you have to play paddles every Sunday? Wouldn't it be fun to sleep in and fool around a little?"

"I need to get out," he said.

"Of what? Get out of what?" I asked.

"The house," he answered.

Blood from a stone, my mother would say when her efforts to win my father's affections failed.

I would hear the car go down the driveway. I'd call my friend Susan.

"What's up?" she said.

"You know that hole in my ego?" I said. "Well, I've fallen in."

"You're great," she'd tell me. "He loves you."

"How do you know?"

"Because I love you. You're very loveable," she'd say.

"That doesn't make any sense, and, besides, you're prejudiced."

When I got off the phone, I'd feel better, hopeful, knowing that when George got home, I'd try again.

In 1982, George and I built a country house together.

It was truly a joint enterprise, and, for the first time in our relationship, we felt like a team. On weekends, we would drive up to the mountains to see how far the contractor had gotten with our project. We'd stand on the beams and measure the rooms. We watched the mason carefully build the fireplace with cobblestones taken from the creek below. I imagined George building a fire on cold, winter nights, us sitting together, having intimate conversations—the fantasy I'd had since that day on the steps in Fire Island. George was excited for the house but filled with trepidation. The stock market didn't cooperate. The market tanked on the day we broke ground. They called it Black Friday. George, to his credit, did not pull the plug on our project, and the building moved ahead.

One summer night, we were standing on the deck of the country house, the sun was setting, and there was a chill in the air. George had his arm around my shoulders. We had been getting along better. I felt safe enough to take the risk. I wanted that proposal I'd never received long ago.

"Ask me to marry you," I said. "I promise I'll say yes. I just would love to hear you say it."

His face was in silhouette, and I couldn't read his expression. He took his arm away and stared out at the mountain. I thought he was formulating the answer. I waited patiently.

"Look at the bats," he said, pointing out the dark shadows swooping through the sky. "They are rodents with wings. Look how close they come—as if they are going to fly directly into your face, making you want to duck for cover. Amazing creatures," he said.

"You're amazing," I said. "Didn't you hear me? Why are you talking about bats?"

"What do you want from me?" he said.

"Didn't you hear me? I just said what I want." I pulled my wedding band off my finger—a ring I'd made for myself from diamonds I'd inherited from my mother. "Here," I said, "put it in a drawer. Do whatever you want with it. It isn't going back on my finger until you propose."

"Suit yourself," he said putting it in his pocket and going back inside the house. The screen door slammed behind him. I stood on the deck and cried. The stars were out, and the bats were gone. The ring stayed in the drawer.

"I'm too demanding," I told my analyst. "I want too much. My mother was right. She always said, 'If I give you a finger, you want a whole hand.' He's a good man. What's my problem?" I said, crying.

"It's not just your needs, Linda. It's also his limitations," she said.

"Am I trying to get blood from a stone?" I asked. She didn't answer.

It took me more than twenty years to realize that George was a gambler—he didn't invest in stocks, he bet on them. He was cautious when he bet his own money at blackjack, but wild when he played the market with other people's money. My friends and colleagues, dazzled by his confident persona and air of authority, readily gave him their savings. In every case, he lost their money. They looked at me as if I had reneged on a promise. I started to keep a low profile and avoid professional gatherings. Despite bad results, those clients kept giving him their money. Like a smooth operator, he was deft at shifting the blame. *Maybe Etienne was right. Maybe I did marry my father.*

He had a large book of business and he was successful for many of his clients but rich, older, male clients were particularly at risk. They became the father George was never able to impress. He felt an undue pressure to prove he was smart and worthy of attention—a man to be admired.

Ah, I thought, *so this is why George was never comfortable at the Director's Council.* Once I saw it, I saw it everywhere, but I also questioned myself. Had I been blind because of all the ways I'd benefited from his misdeeds? I decided that I was no better than a mafia wife enjoying the ill-gotten largesse. We went on adventure vacations all over the world. I bought an Audi and, at my urging, he bought a Jaguar. We bought the Princeton house and built the house in the Catskills. We sent five kids through private schools. How much was paid for with gambling monies?

When George developed a *failsafe* scheme for investing in naked options, I could no longer contain myself. I was sophisticated enough by then to know that naked options were highly volatile—they were not called *naked* for nothing. When they got away from you, they were like renegade horses—almost impossible to rein in.

Herbie Shapiro fit the prototype of the father-man. George convinced him to "invest" in options and trust his strategy. Herbie bet on George, and when George didn't deliver, Herbie got pissed; more than he hated to lose, Herbie hated to be wrong. He brought George to arbitration. Arbitration to a stockbroker is like a malpractice suit to a physician—not good.

George won the arbitration but lost the confidence of his firm. He was put on probation and was not allowed to trade options or commodities. He had a manager who looked the other way as George continued to play the market. Now there was more than his self-esteem on the table; his job was at stake, and a potential civil suit, but the market was going his way, so clients kept bringing in money. George, a bottom fisher, loved to bet on stocks at their low. "A good broker," he said, "is like a fireman. He runs in when everyone else is running out."

He was glib. He was sure of himself. My anxiety increased.

I waited for a commercial break in the Knicks game, handed him a Black Russian, and casually asked, "What's going on at the office?"

"Nothing," he said. "Let me watch the game."

"I'm worried. Why don't we take some of the pressure off, downsize, and reduce our overhead?" I couldn't get his attention.

"Stop worrying," he said patting my hand. "I'm fine. Relax. Let me watch the game."

The brokerage business was changing. The emphasis was on investing in managed money rather than buying individual stocks. *Who Moved My Cheese?* was a gift book to all the attendees at the Council. George and I sat on a chaise by the hotel pool.

"Your cheese moved. You've got to change your game. Enough with betting on stocks, you have to start putting your clients in managed money," I said.

Managed money meant that George could no longer trade stocks on a daily basis. In other words, there would be no *action*.

"And when did you become the maven?" he answered.

I went to a lawyer and drew up papers to put all of our assets in my name.

"It's for our protection," I explained. "I'm not trying to cheat you out of anything. If we get a divorce, the papers state that half of what we own belongs to you, but I can't count on you to protect us."

He began to argue, telling me that I was crazy, and who did I think I was, but I'd come a long way from the woman who'd initially been afraid to strip the wallpaper.

"Don't put me off," I said. "Either you sign or I walk."

He signed, but I paid. Every night he fell asleep in his study. He would wake up and slip under the covers after I'd fallen asleep. I would find him next to me in the morning. In the evenings, as if nothing was wrong, he'd be waiting in the living room, martini in hand, waiting for me to come out of my office. He'd ask about my day. We'd talk without touching.

Over the next few years there was no more talking. We'd sip our drinks in silence. I used every prompt I could to start a conversation, but George would answer my questions with shrugs and grunts. He wasn't just angry, he was depressed. I thought it was a reaction to me and his situation at work, but soon we'd find out that depression was an early sign of pancreatic cancer.

The Thanksgiving after he was diagnosed, all the children and their partners came to dinner. George stood, glass raised.

"Linda always said that she wanted to have time to say goodbye before she died. I always thought I wanted to just keel over," he said, laughing, "but Linda was right, and I'm glad I have this time."

He went around the table, and one by one, told each of the children why he loved them and what they meant to him. He thanked them all for everything they had done for him. I was moved. I loved him so deeply in that moment.

I waited for my turn. What would he say about me? I had done the research and found a clinical trial. I drove him into the city for every chemotherapy appointment, doctor's appointment, blood test, cat scans, pet scans—but my turn never came. He passed me by.

Why do I care? It isn't what matters. Go check the turkey. Forget about it, I told myself.

I slipped away to the kitchen. I didn't want anyone to see my tears. Had they noticed? I hope they hadn't noticed.

Valentine's Day, February 14, 2007, the month before he died. I came out from my office, having seen my last patient. He was sitting at the kitchen table, trying to read the paper, but his eyes were shot from the chemo. He had trouble focusing. I walked up behind him, put my arms around his shoulders and gave him a kiss on his head. He was frail—too tired to shave. His clothes hung off him like a homeless man. It broke my heart to see him this way. He patted my hand.

"Had I been well enough," he said, his voice weak, "I'd planned to go to the jewelry store, buy you a ring, and propose in the way you wished I had before we married"

I was moved. "It's not the ring that counts. I don't need a ring," I said. "You can propose without a ring."

He smiled. I waited. He reached up and gave me a peck on the cheek and went back to reading the paper. Five weeks later he was gone.

One month after he died, when cleaning out his desk I found this card. It said all that I ever wished to hear. Why he hadn't given it to me I will never know.

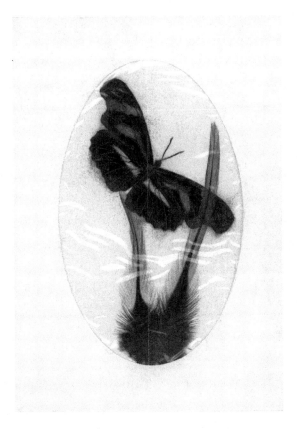

Dearest Linda

While this year doesn't hold much promise of being one of your best ever, it will have some special aspects to it.

This is the year that I —

— recognize all you can and do bring into our lives
— Appreciate your unending care of and for me
— and above all, the year I am most aware of my love for you

Lets make the most of it.
Forever
George

I am sitting on the deck of the country house, drinking a martini. The air is cool and smells of pine. Each evening, I wait for the blue heron to cross the sky, returning to his partner in a nearby lake. He is a devoted and dependable bird. The sun is setting, and the soft gray clouds, shaped like cherubs and dragons, are rimmed in gold.

Inside, there's a fire to be made. I would start with a teepee of logs, just as George had shown me.

∽ the spring line ∾

I look down at the street from my apartment window. Sixteen floors up is not that far down. People walk their dogs—always the dogs, guaranteed to get you outside in the worst weather—trying to juggle their umbrellas, hold on to the leash, and scoop up the poop. The strong wind blows the umbrellas inside out, making the task impossible.

Mounds of dirty snow and slush push up against parked cars—cars covered in snow, like frosted cakes in strange, elongated shapes. A man stands in the street wanting to get to the sidewalk. He walks this way and that, measuring with his eyes, not sure where best to put his feet to climb the mountain.

In New York City, February is not a short month. An unbroken string of gray days blends one into the next. My mood is as clouded as the sky. I've decided, weather or not, I must get out of the house. I must breathe fresh air, even knowing that the cold will make me gasp. I am wary of the ice. Normally I appear to be in charge of my long, lean, seventy-two-year-old body—steady on my feet and purposeful. But since the fall last January, I take mincy little steps, like a child learning how to skate. Steps that are more likely to cause me to slip than the confident strides I took before the fall. I can't help it; I am afraid.

The people at the Pilates studio, where I had just been, heard me fall down the steps. What could that have sounded like? A series of thumps? A scream? A loud groan? I was on the descent in the narrow hallway on the marble steps, between the second floor Pilates studio and the street. They found me head first, lying, I'm told, like a harpooned porpoise, in my gray down coat, my head swimming in blood.

"Linda! Linda!" Their voices were a faint echo from a faraway canyon.

"Linda! Can you hear me?"

That's me, I thought. *I think that's me: Linda. I want to tell them that I smell, I taste iron. Do you smell the iron?* I want to ask.

"Who should we call?" they ask.

I hear myself mumble, "Paul." The man I've been with for three years—the boyfriend, with the big brain and seductive smile. For more than three decades, the correct answer to *who should we call* would've been my husband George.

"What's his number?"

"Favorites," is all I can answer. It is too hard to listen. Harder still to speak. I go back where it is soft and black and fluid.

A siren. Motion. An ambulance? A woman in a uniform holds a bottle on a tube.

"Who should we call?" she shouts.

Why is she yelling? Why is everyone yelling at me?

"Why are you yelling?" I think I say aloud.

"Who should we call?" she yells again.

"David," I whisper.

"Who is David?"

Why so many questions? Leave me alone. I am floating, weightless, in a warm, purple pool.

"My son," I manage to answer.

"What's his number? We need his number."

I am too tired, too far away. I want her to shut up. I come up one more time and remember the number. *Imagine that*, I think.

In a room. I can't move my head. The lights are too bright. Faces without form peer down on me.

"How did you fall?" someone asks.

"I don't know," I groan.

"Where is this?" I ask and I ask, but no one will answer.

"We've told you three times," someone says, "you're in New York Presbyterian Hospital. You fell."

Ah, of course, a place I know well. East Sixty-eighth between York and the river. Valet parking. Chemo lab. *Hello, George. How are you doing?* Stupid question to ask someone with cancer. So many stupid questions.

I am back in 2006—a warm day for the end of March. We are driving up to our country house. Happy. Young friends are coming to join us. George waits in the car while I run in to Citarella's to pick up steaks for the barbecue. When I come out, George is on the phone; he hands it to me. The doctor is at first unwilling to discuss the results over the phone, but I insist. "Pancreatic cancer," she says. *Not good*, I think, but I don't yet know just how bad "not good" is going to be. All I know is that the bottom has just fallen out. We continue to drive, stunned, as if we've just seen a terrible accident on the side of the road.

My grown sons, David and Robbie, are standing at the foot of the bed. Paul is standing there too. For a moment I remember it is Paul, not George, who holds my heart. George has been gone now for too many years. Paul and David and Robbie look like three dwarfs. *What is the name of the dwarf that looks frightened? Was there a dwarf that looked frightened?* I try to ask them but no sound comes out. Robbie is holding his cell phone, taking my picture. I try to smile, but my face won't do what I tell it.

"I want to see the picture," I manage to mutter.

"No, you don't," says Robert.

"Yes, I do." *Why is he arguing? Was there a dwarf who argued?*

David, knowing that I won't be put off, tells Rob to just show me the picture.

It is a picture of a woman. Her face is swollen. Distorted. Rivulets of blood run down her face like red roads on a blue map. Her eye is swollen shut. A tube comes out of her nose. There is a gash across her eyebrow and a brace on her neck. I cannot connect this picture to myself. *I'm sorry*, I say, without speaking, *but I cannot visit with you anymore.* I float away.

I am in the kitchen of our Princeton house, staring at the dishes, trying not to listen to the hollow sound of George's feet falling off each step. He is seventy-nine. It is one year since the day of his diagnosis. The cancer has eaten the inside of his body the way parasites bore into a weakened tree. How humiliating for him to be held up by his sons—one under each arm. They are bringing him down for the last time, but I don't realize yet that it's the last. I should have realized. If I'd known that last night was the last we would sleep together in the same bed, would I have held him tighter? Would I have stayed awake all night just to feel him there? We put the hospital bed in the center of the garden room. If he opens his eyes, he can see the sky or the plantings around the patio. He can watch the tiny buds appear on the trees, harkening a spring he will never see.

"Are you comfortable, George? Would you like another pillow? It's all right. Sleep. I'll be right here." I rest my head on his chest. Using all his strength, he manages to put his arm around my shoulders. I hear myself whimpering. He sleeps.

My head is in a machine.

"Pictures of your brain," someone says.

My brain, I think. *I think with my brain. This can't be good.*

I am in a smaller room. David sits in a chair, his head resting in his hands. Paul is leaning over the bed, holding my hand. I don't see the third dwarf.

"Where am I?" I manage to ask.

"New York Presbyterian Hospital," David says again.

"Yes, but where am I?"

"You answer her, Paul." He passes me off. *Grumpy dwarf.*

"You are in the ICU."

"Oh, that's not so good. What happened?" I ask.

"You fell, Ma. You broke the bones in your face—around your eye. Your brain is bleeding. We are waiting to see if it stops bleeding so they can operate on your face," he says and looks at Paul.

Why are you telling me all this? Who are you talking about?

"I'm tired," I whisper.

"Then go back to sleep. We're here. You can go back to sleep."

"George, the sun is coming up. Wake up sweetheart. Open your eyes. Oh, that's good. And a smile. Would you like some water? No. Just a little. All right. Okay. The boys are coming today. They will all be here soon."

It is time to call hospice. I am relieved that this time has come. I am embarrassed that I am relieved. *See, he nodded yes. He knows. We talked about hospice. Right, honey? See, he nodded again.* Where's the number? I can't find the number. No, it's here. It's under the papers. It's here. I know I put it here.

David and Paul have left. I am in a different room. I am told that my brain has stopped bleeding.

"Are you sure you weren't playing hockey?" The doctor laughs. "The last time I saw an injury like this, the guy got a puck in the face." He laughs again.

Ha! Ha!

"We are going to operate to fix the bones in your face. Don't worry you'll be fine. Just don't laugh."

Ha! Ha!

Why is the hospice nurse sleeping? She is supposed to be awake. Wake up! Do your job! "What is that gesture, sweetheart? Your finger to your lip—is that a kiss? I love you too, darling. I'm going to go upstairs and sleep." I glare at the nurse. "The nurse is going to stay with you."

What if he wasn't saying I love you? What if he was touching his mouth because he was hungry? Oh my God, what if he was hungry? I run downstairs. "Are you hungry? Do you want some applesauce? I'll get you some applesauce. Here. Here. Take a bite." No. No. Okay, then maybe it was meant to be a kiss.

So many rooms—this one, recovery, I think. I open my eyes and see Paul. No, it's not Paul. Yes, it is Paul, but he's flat and pink like a strawberry Gumby.

"What time is it?" I ask. I hear my voice coming from a distant place. I am on a blue moon.

"Three o'clock in the morning."

"Why are you here at three o'clock in the morning? Why are you pink? Why are you pink, Paul?" *Ha! Ha!*

He laughs. *Easy for him to laugh.*

"You are hallucinating," he tells me.

"It's not my fault you're pink," I say.

He tells me to go to sleep and when I wake up and see him tomorrow, he won't be pink.

I am draped over my darling George. Sleeping on his chest. Listening for every breath. The sun is coming up, reflecting off the patio and brightening the day. There's the promise of spring in the air. The birds have begun to sing. I lift my head. He is still breathing. Thank you, God. Another morning. "George, it's morning. See, the sun is rising. Wake up, sweetheart. See the sun. Here, I'll open the sliders, so you can feel the air." I've gone ahead and planted some of the pots early with pansies, and aromatic herbs. So when we open the door, he can smell the rosemary.

Paul leaves, and I wonder if I have hallucinated all of it. *Maybe I didn't fall? Maybe I just dreamt I fell. Maybe I fell and I'm dead. Is this smooth and purple floating place where we go when we die? This blue moon?* I reach up and feel the bandages on my face. The nurse comes in.

"Don't touch your face," she says. "Don't smile and try not to sneeze."

Sneezy? No, this one is not a dwarf. This is not a dream and not death.

How not to sneeze? I've no control over that. I start to cry but I can't make a crying face. It is hard to have a straight-faced cry.

"George! George! George!" I'm screaming as I feel him moving farther away.

"No!" he shouts. "No!" The last word he says.

And I know with that *no*, he wants to leave, and he needs me to let him go. His head drops to his shoulder. He looks like a fallen eagle. I put my hand on his foot and follow the heat as it travels up his body. I fist my hand into his armpit— the last warm place. As the energy leaves his body, his face relaxes, and, as if a magician had lifted a veil, a young handsome man appears.

"I am sorry to hear about your husband," a neighbor says. "How are you doing?" Stupid questions but I know people mean well.

"All right," I say politely. "Thank you for asking."

When I leave the hospital, my face is black and blue and swollen. My left eye droops like a basset hound's. The red, lower lid hangs down. I look grotesque—a female Quasimodo. I wear dark glasses even in the house, afraid of my own reflection.

Dr. Elahi has a reputation as a miracle worker, an ocular plastic surgeon. I've never heard of this—two sub-specialties blended into one. I think that such a specialty must have been devised only for me and for hockey players.

Dr. Elahi reassures me that I will look fine when he's done. He operates once and then again. My lower lid is back up near my eye. I look in the mirror. It is almost me again.

"How did you fall?" my neighbor asks.

"I slipped on a slick, wet step," I say, finally remembering.

Now, on the year anniversary of my plummet down those stairs, I look out the window and keep checking the temperature. It is not warm enough yet for the ice to have melted. I am still afraid to go out, but I'm also determined. I have to buy yogurt and coffee. I have to make lunch dates with friends. I have to live.

I put on the high boots with the combat heels—the best boots for snow and ice. The boots that shouldn't have slipped off the step, but they did. They are still the best boots I own. I put on the gray down coat that kept me from breaking all the bones in my body. I've cleaned the blood off the coat. I zip the zipper and snap the snaps. *Was it zipped when I fell? It must have been zipped. Did they take it off before they put me in the ambulance or when I got to the emergency room? Why does it matter? Just put on the damn coat and get out of the house.*

In the pocket is only one glove. *Where's the other glove?* It's too cold to go out without the glove. They are fleece-lined, black, suede, warm gloves. *Was I wearing them when I fell? When did I last wear the gloves?* I can't remember.

I'm getting increasingly frantic. If I find the glove, I won't fall again. The gloves, two, one for each hand, will protect me. I go through the drawers. I look in the closet. I can't find the damn glove. I call the nurse who took care of me when I came home from the hospital.

"Nadine, my glove?" I ask her.

"No gloves," she says, "I didn't see any gloves."

There were no gloves!

I'm on my own. Right, baby? You're gone. Somewhere in the stratosphere, somewhere on a blue planet, somewhere near the sun. Are you omniscient now? Can you help me find the glove? It is an empty prayer, yet in the hospital, he felt so close.

I try to reassure myself, glove or no glove, George or no George, my life has gone on. There is Paul, after all, but I'm convinced that only those gloves will protect me. I give up looking, and decide to replace them. I bought them at Harry's on Broadway and 84th Street, thirteen blocks away. Thirteen is a very unlucky number. My father told me to be particularly careful on Friday 13. What day is today? The month is February 2015. The calendar tells me that it's not Friday, nor is it the thirteenth. I'm relieved.

Bundled up, I take to the streets. I watch my steps with

the vigilance of an inspector looking for clues after an accident. I try to walk in the wake of the man in front of me—his
step, my step. If he doesn't fall, I won't fall. I'm terrified of
black ice. It masquerades as wet sidewalk worse than glass.
It fools you and lands you flat on your ass. I am so intent on
looking down that I forget to notice red lights. A cab honks. A
car rushes by and splatters me with slush. Harry's is still one
block ahead.

The window is full of winter boots on sale. The shelves
inside are lined with spring and summer shoes. Sandals with
wraparound ties. Canvas shoes in candy stripes, strawberry
and orange, lime green and yellow. Purple-and-lavender flip-
flops. *Are they crazy? Why don't they look outside?*

They do not have the gloves. "Sold out," they tell me. I
begin to panic.

"Please check in the back."

"No gloves. I'm sorry," she says. "Everything we are
stocking now is for spring."

Before I venture back out, to distract myself, I walk up
and down the rows with the spring line of footwear. I pick
out several pair to try on. Retail therapy. It will be risky carrying packages while trying to stay upright—like the dog
walkers with their poop bags and inside-out umbrellas—but I
can manage it. It's then that I realize I've just walked thirteen
blocks in New York winter without falling, and with only one
glove. Clearly, I'm able to stand on my own two feet.

"Can I see this pair in an eight?" I say.

⌒ acknowledgments ⌒

This book is dedicated with love to my husband, George Wolfgang, who died March 27, 2007.

It could have not been written without Melanie Bishop. Her intelligence, creativity, and unwavering support helped me to get up each morning and face the terror of the blank page.

I would also like to thank Mindy Lewis and the members of our writing workshop for the multiple reads of the same material until, with their help, I finally got it right. And thanks are due to Philip Lopate, the members of the NYWI summer writing retreat, and to Mindy Greenstein who also attended the workshop and has since become a friend and reader of my work. Her feedback is always spot on.

Gratitude to Nancy McWilliams and Ghislaine Boulanger for their kindness and caring. It is their expertise that helped me navigate the road between trauma and trust, grief and acceptance. They have given me the courage to accept myself—a prerequisite for writing this memoir.

Thanks to family and friends, some of them readers, but all of them supporters of my efforts to complete this book: Lucy James, Renee and Jack Crary, Robert Yeager, Joan Odes,

Joan Morgan, Caitlin Thomas, David Clark, Roni Natov, Amy Lerner, Richard Skolnik, Vickie and Steve Morris, Susan Held, Darcy Tromanhauser, and Gus Hinojosa.

With much love and gratitude to my cousin Louise who, no matter what, has always been there for me.

A special thanks to Paul Bloom who not only read every chapter but also sat patiently while I read each word aloud. His critique definitely made this a better book.

A special thanks to my daughter-in-law Kim Johnson for her belief in my writing and her willingness to share my work with her friends.

To my son Jonathan Munk, a poet and an editor, who many times helped me find the right word, restructure the wrong sentence, and remove the misplaced comma.

To my assistant Jonathan Young, who has patiently helped me navigate the new world of social media.

To the team at She Writes Press for supporting me through this project and for their dedication to closing the gender gap in publishing.

To Angelle Barbazon and the team at JKS for helping me spread the word.

And thanks to all of the following:

To Thomas and Randall at Vagabond's House, for always finding me the right chair.

To the editors at *Alligator Juniper* and *Post Road*, for publishing two chapters of this book, helping me to believe that it deserved to be in print.

"The Flowers" first appeared in *Alligator Juniper*, 2016

"The Spring Line" first appeared in *Post Road*, 2016

∽ about the author ∽

L inda I. Meyers is a psychologist and psychoanalyst in New York City and Princeton, NJ. She has been published in professional journals and academic books. In 2016, she published two chapters from her memoir, *The Tell*: "The Flowers," a top five finalist in *Alligator Juniper's* annual contest in creative nonfiction, and "The Spring Line" in *Post Road*. She lives in New York City.

Author photo © Dylan/Patric Photographer

∽ selected titles from she writes press ∽

She Writes Press is an independent publishing company founded to serve women writers everywhere. Visit us at www.shewritespress.com.

The Butterfly Groove: A Mother's Mystery, A Daughter's Journey by Jessica Barraco. $16.95, 978-1-63152-800-2. In an attempt to solve the mystery of her deceased mother's life, Jessica Barraco retraces the older woman's steps nearly forty years earlier—and finds herself along the way.

A Different Kind of Same: A Memoir by Kelley Clink. $16.95, 978-1-63152-999-3. Several years before Kelley Clink's brother hanged himself, she attempted suicide by overdose. In the aftermath of his death, she traces the evolution of both their illnesses, and wonders: If he couldn't make it, what hope is there for her?

The Beauty of What Remains: Family Lost, Family Found by Susan Johnson Hadler. $16.95, 978-1-63152-007-5. Susan Johnson Hadler goes on a quest to find out who the missing people in her family were—and what happened to them—and succeeds in reuniting a family shattered for four generations.

All the Ghosts Dance Free: A Memoir by Terry Cameron Baldwin. $16.95, 978-1-63152-822-4. A poetic memoir that explores the legacy of alcoholism and teen suicide in one woman's life—and her efforts to create an authentic existence in the face of that legacy.

Scattering Ashes: A Memoir of Letting Go by Joan Rough. $16.95, 978-1-63152-095-2. A daughter's chronicle of what happens when she invites her alcoholic and emotionally abusive mother to move in with her in hopes of helping her through the final stages of life—and her dream of mending their tattered relationship fails miserably.

Times They Were A-Changing: Women Remember the '60s & '70s edited by Kate Farrell, Amber Lea Starfire, and Linda Joy Myers. $16.95, 978-1-938314-04-9. Forty-eight powerful stories and poems detailing the breakthrough moments experienced by women during the '60s and '70s.

Printed in the United States
by Baker & Taylor Publisher Services